Contents

KU-526-130

Introduction	5
Imitated Pronunciation	5
Brief Background to Germany	7
Traditional Festivals and Entertainment	13
Social Habits and Customs	18
Public notices	16
Useful everyday words and phrases	19
Days of the week, months, seasons	25
Numbers	26
Time	28
Colours	29
Hotels	30
Useful words and phrases	29
Camping and Caravanning	35
Useful words and phrases	36
Motoring	39
Rule of the road, parking	40
Right of way, speed limits	41
Translation of road signs	42
Useful words and phrases	44
Public Transport	50
By Rail	50
Useful words and phrases	51
By Coach, River Steamer	55

Useful words and phrases	56
By Air	58
Useful words and phrases	59

Food and Wine 61
North Germany	61
Central Germany	62
Bavaria	63
The wine label	63
Useful words and phrases	64

Shopping 70
Useful words and phrases—general	71
Chemists	75
Hairdressers	77
Photographic shop	79
Other Shops	80

Sport, The Beach 81
| Useful words and phrases | 82 |

Post Office, Telephones 84
| Useful words and phrases | 85 |

Medical Services 87
| Useful words and phrases | 87 |

Useful Information 90
Currency, Banks, Tipping	90
Tourist Offices	91
Public Conveniences	92
Clothing sizes	93
Conversion tables	94

HUGO'S
GERMAN
PHRASE BOOK

Published by

Hugo's Language Books Limited

104 JUDD STREET, LONDON, WC1H 9NF

FIRST PUBLISHED 1970

© 1970 Hugo's Language Institute Ltd.

ISBN: 085285 005 0

Latest reprint 1979

Facts and figures given in this book were correct when printed. If you discover any changes, please write to us.

Printed in Great Britain by The Anchor Press Ltd, Tiptree, Essex

Introduction

This is primarily a phrase book in which selections of everyday words and phrases, complete with imitated pronunciation, are grouped under the usual headings of "Hotel", "Motoring", "Shopping" and so on. There are also conversion tables for weights, measures, distances, tyre pressures and clothing sizes.

In addition to the general notes that accompany each heading, there is more detailed information on German history, regions, social habits, traditional festivals, food and wine. It sometimes happens that the tourist, despite his excellent intentions, causes both himself and his host unnecessary embarrassment by committing some innocent breach of local custom or etiquette. We hope that this book will enable you to avoid making such mistakes, as well as helping you to make yourself understood.

THE IMITATED PRONUNCIATION

When reading the imitated pronunciation, the syllable marked by an acute accent (´) must be stressed. Pronounce each syllable as if it formed part of an English word and you will be understood sufficiently well. The exact sound can be more nearly obtained by remembering the following points:

ow is to be pronounced as in **"cow"** or **"how"**.

EE is like the French **u** sound (resembling the English **ee** in **"seen"**, pronounced with rounded lips).

e   (roman) must be pronounced like e in **"open"** or a in **"local"**.

g   must always be pronounced as in **"go"** or **"drag"**.

k   (roman) is given a guttural sound as in the Scottish **"loch"**.

r   (roman) must not be pronounced at all; it is there merely to ensure the correct pronunciation of the preceding vowel.

s   at the end of a word or syllable sounds like the ss in **"missing"**. At the beginning of a word or syllable it is softer, rather like s in **"easy"**.

When unimportant words like **der, das,** form part of a sentence, the vowel sound they contain is hardly heard. We therefore imitate them as *der, duss* (about rhyming with the second syllable in **"water"**, **"circus"**). But as isolated words they are pronounced *dare, dahss*.

Instead of putting the definite or indefinite article before nouns in the vocabulary we have given the gender only. This will enable you to precede the noun with either "a" or "the", depending on the prevailing circumstances. The notes on page 22 will help you further.

A Brief Background to Germany

The Federal Republic of Germany, with which this book is concerned, is generally known as West Germany and has the university city of Bonn as its capital. Berlin, the old German capital, lies beyond the Iron Curtain in East Germany (the Democratic Republic) and since 1948 has been divided into West and East Berlin – with the infamous Wall marking this partition even more sharply in recent years. West Berlin has the same legal, financial and economic system (and therefore the same currency) as the Federal Republic.

West Germany has an area of 95,744 square miles and a population of about 57 million. It comprises the following Länder (with their capitals shown in brackets): Bavaria (Munich), Baden-Württemberg (Stuttgart), Saarland (Saarbrücken), North Rhine-Westphalia (Düsseldorf), Lower Saxony (Hannover), Schleswig-Holstein (Kiel), Hesse (Wiesbaden), Rhineland-Palatinate (Mainz), and the free cities of Hamburg and Bremen.

The northern part of the country is a large plain with very few uplands, and is generally disregarded by the majority of visitors. But its ports and cosmopolitan cities, with their magnificent architecture and accumulation of art treasures, make it a highly interesting region. Along the deeply indented Baltic coastline of Schleswig-Holstein are thickly wooded hills and lush meadowland with placid lakes. Picturesque fishing villages are scattered along the

7

North Sea coast, and the Lüneberg Heath which extends between the Elbe and the Aller includes a large nature reserve. Though most visitors to this region make for the coastal resorts, a tour along the central reaches of the river Weser or in East Friesland can be equally rewarding, although much quieter.

The central region is dominated by wooded uplands, with ancient towns, moated castles and manor houses, stately farmsteads and Romanesque churches. Between the rivers Lippe and Ruhr is the Westphalian section of the great industrial area of the Ruhr. The Harz mountains are renowned for climbing and winter sports. South of the Weserbergland is the Electorate of Hesse, which includes the wine growing areas along the Rhine and Main rivers.

The Rhine rises in the Alps and wends its way northward, an international highway in the heart of Europe. It flows between the Black Forest and the Vosges Mountains and cuts a narrow winding passage through the Rhenish Slate Mountains. It is joined on the east bank by the river Main, dividing the Odenwald from the Taunus and the Rheingau, some of the finest wine-growing districts in Germany. From the Moselle (Mosel), with its many vineyards, to the lower Rhine region, dotted with fairytale castles, stretch the Eifel Mountains; these are rich in lovely villages and hamlets secluded from the beaten track. Wherever the banks of the Rhine (over half-a-mile wide at Mainz and narrowing to 370 feet where it flows past the famous Lorelei Rock) face the sun and are protected from the cold winds, terraced vineyards climb the slopes, giving ground only to romantic castles, villages

8

and inns. The entire region deserves a lasting place in the affections of all those travellers who have had the good fortune to go by steamer up the Rhine.

Baden-Württemberg is a hospitable country with ancient towns, modern cities and many spas and health resorts. Lake Constance (Bodensee), situated on the borders of Germany, Austria and Switzerland, is the centre of a tourist region rich in works of art. The Black Forest (Schwarzwald) is well known and loved by tourists from all over the world, and at the southern edge is the Hegau, the Upper Rhine district and the Kaiserstuhl massif, famous for its vintages. In Württemberg, the deep-cut valley of the Danube divides the Swabian Alb from Upper Swabia and both these somewhat neglected districts offer a wealth of attractions, ranging from magnificent examples of Swabian baroque architecture to stalactite-filled caves. Though much of the landscape is austere and rocky, it is a hiker's paradise. The gentle hills of the Kraichgau, the southern end of the Bergstrasse, and the Madonnenländchen on the eastern edge of the Odenwald are still waiting to be explored by those who wish to leave the popular well-trodden routes.

Bavaria is the country of traditional songs and dances, ancient customs and costumes, and a people who love the pleasures of the table and the gaiety of social gatherings. Upper Bavaria, and, further west, the Allgäu, are dominated by the peaks of the northern Alps. Here there are precipices and waterfalls, glens and glaciers, chamois, eagles, deer and marmots. The fertile grain-growing district of Lower Bavaria adjoins East Bavaria, which reaches its greatest height in the primitive rocks of the Bavarian and upper Palatine Forests. East Bavaria links up with Franconia; here are limestone caves and extensive woods, and the mighty ridge of the Fichtel Mountains. The ancient towns and villages abound with architectural wonders and works of art, the castle-topped crags enchant the tourist, and there are many fashionable spas and secluded summer resorts providing a warm hospitality.

Berlin, since World War II, has been the gateway connecting the west with the east, and a sightseeing tour of West and East Berlin is an unforgettable experience because of the contrasting scenes it reveals. A new western centre has developed near the Zoo Station, around the Kaiser Wilhelm Memorial Church, and everywhere are new buildings, outstanding in design. Twenty theatres give Berlin a leading position in the theatrical world. The performances of the Berlin Philharmonic Orchestra are highlights of the concert season. West Berlin is endowed with beautiful surroundings, particularly Lake Wannsee with its much frequented beach. There are excellent communications by road, rail and air between West Berlin and the Federal Republic. For the road or rail journey, foreign visitors require a transit visa which is obtainable at the interzonal frontier points, and a proper passport (see page 40).

History

When the Roman Empire collapsed the Franks became the most important tribe in Germany. By the year

00 they also controlled all France and northern Italy.
Known as the Holy Roman Empire, this area was ruled
by Charlemagne, the Frankish king. As can be imagined,
unity was hard to maintain in an empire of such differing
peoples after Charlemagne's death, although Frederick I
(1155–90) was notably successful in this respect.

Towards the end of the 13th century the various
princes, barons and cities became more autonomous, with
the emperor being chosen by seven "Electors". The 14th
century saw the formation of the Hanseatic League by
several northern cities; this early form of common market
was very powerful throughout northern Europe.

In the 15th century the Hapsburgs, from Austria,
took the throne and slowly the Catholic influence increased. In 1517 Luther broke with the Catholic Church;
this resulted in the Peasants' Revolt and increased the
Protestant princes' desire for independence. A century
later all Germany was in the grip of the Thirty Years War,
which ended in victory for the Protestant princes and
cities over the Catholic emperor and his followers.

From the end of the Thirty Years War Prussia grew
both in size and military strength, which was achieved by
cunning diplomacy and total religious toleration, a
sentiment unknown in the 17th century. This movement
continued until the time of Bismarck when Brandenburg-
Prussia engulfed Germany. The most important figure of
the 18th century was Frederick the Great of Prussia
(which lately had been the Electorate of Brandenburg).
In 1792 Prussia and Austria joined forces against France,
but were beaten by Napoleon; in 1806 the Holy Roman
Empire, such as it was, ceased to exist.

Although the French were driven out a few years later, it was not until after the Revolution in 1848 that real unity returned to Germany. By 1870 they were once again at war with France and emerged victorious, with Bismarck and the Prussian faction even more dominant among the now federated German states. In 1888 Wilhelm II dismissed Bismarck and began a rearmament policy that led up to the 1914–18 war.

After the treaty of Versailles in 1919, the Weimar republic began its short life; Hindenburg, his government weakened by the global economic crisis, handed over to the Nazis in 1933. Hitler assumed complete power, and annexed both Austria and Czechoslovakia before marching on Poland. This started the 1939–45 war, after which the country was divided into four zones of military occupation (British, French, American and Russian) with Berlin similarly split up. German territory east of the Oder–Neisse line went to Poland. In 1948–49, with relations between the Russians and the Western alliance at flashpoint, the latter negotiated with survivors of the old Weimar republic to form a government. This gave birth to the present Federal Republic, which achieved complete independence in 1955.

Facts and Figures

Germany has contributed a great deal to the world's store of artistic and musical treasures, and to material wealth also. The soaring Gothic buildings, intricate wood carving and beautiful stained glass, book-printing as a result of Gutenberg's inventions; these mark the achievements of the 13th, 14th and 15th centuries. During the

Renaissance period such artists as Dürer and Holbein the Younger flourished, and Martin Luther brought about important theological reforms.

In the 16th and 17th centuries, as in France, great palaces with landscaped parks were built for princes and barons; the famous Meissen porcelain dates from this time. Bach, one of the most prolific composers, wrote his wonderful church music; Goethe and Schiller contributed greatly to literature. Famous names of the 19th century are Beethoven, Brahms and Wagner (music), Diesel (engines), Röntgen (physics), and Karl Marx, the father of revolutionary socialism.

The industrial revolution affected Germany as it did other European countries, and today about half the population works in industry; the Ruhr complex of steel and chemical works is one of the greatest in the world. Farming is small by comparison, and West Germany has to import a large amount to feed her dense population.

Traditional Festivals and Entertainment

Many of the festivals celebrated throughout the year are rooted in ancient traditions, and beautiful old peasant costumes are often worn on these occasions, especially where the traditional way of life is still adhered to in country villages. The gaiety of carnival time is matched by the time-honoured ceremonies of welcoming Spring and driving out Winter.

13

The fame of German harvest and vintage festivals is widespread, and the first tapping of "March ale" and "May bock" are great occasions. Fishermen, woodcutters, alpine shepherds and huntsmen also maintain their own traditional festivals. Then there are the great religious festivals celebrated throughout the length and breadth of the country – Christmas in Germany is something that has to be experienced to be truly understood. Everywhere the visitor is welcomed as a friend to enjoy the spirit of carnival and devotion.

The most famous of the many Rhineland wine festivals is the Dürkheimer Wurstmarkt, which means Sausage Fair. In August there are illuminations and fireworks on the Rhine from Braubach to Koblenz, but the most impressive "Rhine Aflame" spectacle is in September, at St. Goarshausen beneath the Lorelei Rock and at St. Goar on the opposite bank.

Munich's Beer Festival or Oktoberfest is from mid-September to early October; during the Fasching carnival the most sedate and solid citizens can be seen leaving their offices dressed like clowns and making for the nearest source of amusement (and beer).

To list only a short selection of the many colourful festivals there are: International May Festival at Wiesbaden; the Ruhr Festival at Recklinghausen (early summer); plays and operas performed in the traditional setting of the ruined convent at Bad Hersfeld; Garden Serenades at Hannover-Herrenhausen (July–August); the Music Festival at Kassel during October; a Canaries' Singing Contest at Hohegeiss and St. Andreasberg on

Midsummer Day; the Pied Piper of Hamelin Festival (June, September).

Many trade fairs, exhibitions and sample fairs are held throughout the year. Those at Frankfurt/Main and Cologne are held in the spring and autumn, and others take place in: Berlin (industrial and agricultural, the International Film Festival in June and the Festival Weeks during September); Nuremberg (the famous Toys Fair); Offenbach (leather goods); Munich (handicrafts); Hannover (industrial). Düsseldorf, Essen, Hamburg, Saarbrücken, Stuttgart and Wiesbaden also hold trade fairs of one sort or another.

N.B. "CALENDAR OF EVENTS" is published by the German National Tourist Association and the various official local and regional tourist offices. It contains the dates and details of all these annual traditional, theatrical, musical, commercial and sporting events. Copies can be obtained from the German National Tourist Office, 61 Conduit Street, London W.1.

Do remember to confirm dates, hours of opening (museums, etc.) if you intend making a special journey; local conditions might result in an event being cancelled at the last minute – especially in winter.

Theatre and Music

The standard of theatrical productions and music throughout the Federal Republic and in West Berlin is generally high. There are ten theatres in Berlin and the world-famous Berlin Philharmonic Orchestra gives regular performances. Bonn stages a festival of Beethoven's works every few years. Würzburg has a Mozart Festival during June, and during July–August there is the great Wagner Festival at Bayreuth – the oldest German opera festival.

The most famous of all drama festivals is perhaps the Passion Play at Oberammergau. This is now acted every decade, although the villagers originally vowed to depict the Passion each year, in thanks for being delivered of a plague in the 17th century. There are three performances a week, each one lasting the whole day, with an interval of two hours at noon.

Casinos

In some German spas and health resorts, State-licensed casinos have been established. These are located at Baden-Baden, Bad Dürkheim, Garmisch-Partenkirchen, Bad Homburg v.d. Höhe, Bad Kissingen, Konstanz and Lindau (Lake Constance), Bad Neuenahr, Bad Reichenhall, Travemünde, Westerland (Sylt), Bad Wiessee, and Wiesbaden. Roulette and baccarat are the most popular games.

Social Habits and Customs

The Germans love to use titles, even the most obscure ones, so when addressing anyone whose position you are aware of, call him Herr Doktor, Herr Professor, Herr Direktor, or whatever he may be. When requesting information from a stranger always preface your request with the words "Verzeihen Sie" (pronounced *fair-tsy'-en see*). Where "Mr" or "Mrs" would be used in English, "Herr" (*hairr*) and "Frau" (*frow*) are used. The equivalent of the polite "Madam" is "Gnädige Frau" (*g'nayd'-ik-e frow*); if you know she is unmarried "Gnädiges Fräulein" (*g'nayd'-ik-ess froy'-line*) is used. "Fräulein" is also used with shop assistants, waitresses, and so on.

Shake hands whenever you meet a friend or make your departure, and though it is not customary to kiss in public, many Germans still indulge in the old-world gallantry of kissing a lady's hand. The gentleman always walks on the lady's left hand side, even though this may mean that she is nearest the edge of the pavement. Sunday is still "best suit" day.

If you are invited to anybody's home, always take your hostess a little gift of flowers or chocolates (which in Germany are very good). You will find that as in most continental countries the children are doted on, and if you would win the immediate esteem of the proud parent, be a child lover.

In business the German believes in brevity, so if you make a phone call you should give your name and immediately come to the point. Socially he is very different; if you are seated next to a stranger in a restaurant he will be eager to talk to you. But avoid discussing 20th century politics. If you order chicken and find no knife and fork, don't worry; it is correct to use your fingers. If you are having drinks at the table, the waitress puts a tick on your beer mat for each drink you order and charges you as you leave.

A knowledge of public notices is desirable since most of them will directly concern you. Here are some of the more common ones.

Ausgang
Exit

Besetzt
Engaged

Damen
Ladies

Eingang
Entrance

Erkundigung einziehen *or* **Auskunft geben**
Information

Est ist verboten, das Gras zu betreten
Keep off the grass

Frei
Vacant

Frisch gestrichen
Wet paint

Geschlossen
Closed

Herren
Gentlemen

Kein Eingang
No entry

Notausgang
Emergency exit

Offen
Open

Privat
Private

Rauchen verboten
No smoking

Stossen
Push

Streng verboten
Strictly forbidden

Trinkwasser
Drinking water

Wagen abstellen verboten *or* **Parken verboten**
No Parking

Ziehen
Pull

Useful Everyday Words and Phrases

about etwa, ungefähr *et'-vah, oon'-ge-fair*
above über, oben EE'-*ber, ohb'-en*
across kreuzweise *kroyts'-vyze*
after nach *nahk*
again wieder *vee'-der*
all alles *ahll'-es*

at an, auf *ahnn, owf*
before vor, bevor *for, be-for'*
behind hinter *hin'-ter*
beneath unter, unten *oonnt'-er, oonnt'-en*
between dazwischen *dah-tsvish'-en*
big gross *grohss*
by bei, an *by, ahnn*
cold kalt *kahlt*
down unten, hinunter *oonnt'-en, hinn-oont'-er*
drink trinken *trink'-en*
early früh *frrEE*
enough genug *gen-ook'*
everybody jedermann *yaid'-er-mahnn*
everything jedes, alles *yaid'-es, ahll'-ess*
everywhere überall *EEb'-er-all*
far weit *vite*
fast schnell *shnell*
food Speise, *f.* Lebensmittel, *pl. shpy'*-ze, *layb'-ens-mit-el*
good gut *goot*
here hier *heer*
high hoch *hohk*
hot heiss *hice*
how many wieviele *vee'-feel-e*
how much wieviel *vee'-feel*
in, into in *inn*
inside drinnen *drinn'-en*
left links *links*
less weniger *vain'-ig-er*
like gleich, ähnlich *glyk, ayn'-lik*
little klein *kline*
lost verloren *fair-lohr'-en*

20

many viele *feel'*-e
nine mein, meine, meiner *mine, mine'*-e, *mine'*-er
more mehr *mair*
near nahe *nah'*-he
no nein *nine*
open offen *off'*-en
to open öffnen, aufmachen *erf'*-nen, *owf'*-mahk-en
outside aussen *owss'*-en
please bitte *bitt'*-e
right rechts *rekts*
slow langsam *lahng'*-zahm
some etwas *et'*-vahs
somebody jemand *yay'*-mahnt
something etwas *et'*-vahs
soon bald *bahlt*
there dort *dohrt*
this dieser, diese, dieses *dees'*-er, *dees'*-e, *dees'*-ess
those diejenigen *dee'*-yayn-ee-gen
through durch *doork*
too many zuviele *tsoo'*-feel-e
too much zuviel *tsoo'*-feel
under unter *oon'*-ter
until bis *bis*
up auf, aufwärts *owf, owf'*-vairts
very sehr *sair*
well wohl, gut *vohl, goot*
when wann, als *vahnn, ahls*
where wo, wohin *voh, voh-in'*
why warum *vah-room'*
without ohne *oh'n*e
yes ja *yah*

21

"A", "an" or "one" is translated **ein** (pronounced *ine*) before masculine and neuter nouns, and **eine** (*ine'*-e) before feminine nouns.

"The" is translated **der** (*der*) before masculine singular nouns, and **das** (*duss*) before neuters. Before feminine singular nouns, use **die** (*de*); this same word is used before plural nouns of all genders.

There are exceptions to the above, but it is as well not to worry about these. It is beyond the scope of this book to go too deeply into grammatical matters.

Thank you	Danke schön
dahngk-e sheᴦn	
Could you direct me to . . . ?	Können Sie mir bitte zeigen wo . . . ?
Keᴦn'-en zee meer bitt'-e tsy'-gen voh	
I don't understand	Ich verstehe nicht
ik fair-shtay'-e nikt	
Do you speak English?	Sprechen Sie englisch?
shprek'-en zee eng'-lish	
I cannot speak German	Ich kann nicht deutsch sprechen
ik kahn nikt doytsh sprek'-en	
Would you please speak slowly?	Würden Sie bitte langsam sprechen?
ᴠEEᴦd'-en zee bitt'-e lahng'-zahm sprek'-en	
Where can I get a . . . ?	Wo bekomme ich ein (eine) . . . ?
voh be-komme' ik ine (ine-e)	

22

Please write it down   Schreiben Sie es bitte auf
       shry'-ben zee ess bit'-e owf

How much is it?   Wieviel kostet das?
       vee-feel' kost'-et duss

Is this enough?   Ist das genug?
       ist duss ge-noogk'

I am very sorry   Es tut mir sehr leid
       ess toot meer zair lite

Have you anything cheaper?   Haben Sie nicht etwas
       billigeres?
       hahb'-en zee nikt et'-vahs bill'-ee-ge-ress

It is very good   Das ist sehr gut
       duss ist zair goot

Have you a list of excursions?   Haben Sie ein Verzeichnis
       von den Ausflügen?
       hahb'-en zee ine fair-tsyk'-niss fon dehn ows'-flEE-gen

How long does it take to . . . ?   Wie lange dauert es bis
       zu . . . ?
       vee lahng'-e dow'-ert ess bis tsoo

We are in a hurry   Wir sind in Eile
       veer sint in i'-le

I have no time   Ich habe keine Zeit
       ik hah'-be kine-e tsite

What is the correct time, please?   Wie spät ist es jetzt genau?
       vee shpayt ist yetst gen-ow'

What is the date today?   Welches Datum haben wir
       heute?
       vel'-kes daht'-oom hahb'-en veer hoyt'-e

How long are you staying?   Wie lange bleiben Sie?
       vee lahng'-e bly'-ben zee

When are you leaving?   Wann gehen (fahren) Sie
                             fort?
  vahnn gay'-en (fahr'-en) zee forht

It is getting late   Es wird schon spät
  ess veert shohn shpayt

Don't be late   Komm (Kommen Sie) nicht
                             spät
  komm (komm'-en zee) nikt shpayt

Good morning (afternoon) Guten Morgen (Tag)
  goot'-en mohr'-gen (tahg)

Goodnight   Gute Nacht
  goot'-e nakt

Goodbye   Auf Wiedersehn
  owf vee'-der-say-en

How are you?   Wie geht es Ihnen?
  vee gayt ess een'-en

Your good health!   Auf Ihr Wohl!
  owf eer vohl

Look   Sieh mal, *or* sehen Sie mal
  zee mahl, zay'-en zee mahl

What is that?   Was ist das?
  vahs ist duss

I have lost my . . .   Ich habe mein . . . verloren
  ik hah'-be mine . . . fair-lohr'-en

This is incorrect   Das stimmt nicht
  duss shtimmt nikt

**I do not wish to speak to Ich will nicht mit Ihnen
you**   (Dir) sprechen
  ik vill nikt mit een'-en (deer) shprek'-en

Go away   Geh fort
  gay fort

I enjoyed myself immensely Ich habe mich grossartig
amüsiert
*ik hah'-be mik grohs'-art-ik ah-*mEE*-seert'*

We enjoyed ourselves Wir haben uns grossartig
immensely amüsiert
*veer hah'-ben oonns grohs'-art-ik ah-*mEE*-seert'*

Thank you for your Vielen Dank für Ihre
hospitality Gastfreundschaft
*feel'-en dahngk f*EER *eer'-e gahsst'-froynt-shahfft*

DAYS OF THE WEEK, MONTHS AND SEASONS

Sunday Sonntag *zonn'-tahg*
Monday Montag *mohn'-tahg*
Tuesday Dienstag *deenss'-tahg*
Wednesday Mittwoch *mit'-vok*
Thursday Donnerstag *donn'-ers-tahg*
Friday Freitag *fry'-tahg*
Saturday Sonnabend (*or* Samstag)
zonn'-ahb-ent (*zahms'-tahg*)

January Januar *yahn'-oo-ahr*
February Februar *fay'-broo-ahr*
March März *mairts*
April April *ahp-ril'*
May Mai *my*
June Juni *yoo'-nee*
July Juli *yoo'-lee*
August August *ow-goost'*
September September *sept-em'-ber*

October Oktober *oct-o'-ber*
November November *noh-vem'-ber*
December Dezember *deh-tsem'-ber*

Spring Frühling *m. fr*EE*-ling*
Summer Sommer *m. zomm'-er*
Autumn Herbst *m. hairpst*
Winter Winter *m. vint'-er*

Christmas Weihnachten *vy'-nahkt-en*
New Year's Day Neujahr *noy'-yar*
Easter Ostern *ohst'-ern*
Whitsun Pfingsten *pfing'-sten*

NUMBERS

1 eins *ines*		**8** acht *ahkt*	
2 zwei *tsvy*		**9** neun *noyn*	
3 drei *dry*		**10** zehn *tsayn*	
4 vier *feer*		**11** elf *elf*	
5 fünf *f*EE*nf*		**12** zwölf *tsverlf*	
6 sechs *sex*		**13** dreizehn *dry'-tsayn*	
7 sieben *seeb'-en*		**14** vierzehn *feer'-tsayn*	

15	fünfzehn *fEEnf'-sayn*	**90**	neunzig *noyn'-sik*
16	sechzehn *sek'-sayn*	**100**	hundert *hoond'-ert*
17	siebzehn *seep'-sayn*	**200**	zweihundert *tsvyhoond'-ert*
18	achtzehn *akt'-sayn*	**1000**	ein Tausend *ine towz'-ent*
19	neunzehn *noyn'-sayn*	**2000**	zwei Tausend *tsvy towz'-ent*
20	zwanzig *tsvahnt'-sik*		
21	einundzwanzig *ine'-oont-tsvant-sik*	**1st**	erste *air'-ste*
22	zweiundzwanzig *tsvy'-oont-tsvant-sik*	**2nd**	zweite *tsvy'-te*
30	dreissig *dry'-sik*	**3rd**	dritte *dritt'-e*
40	vierzig *feer'-sik*		
50	fünfzig *fEEnf'-sik*	$\frac{1}{4}$	ein Viertel *ine feer'-tel*
60	sechzig *sek'-sik*	$\frac{1}{3}$	ein Drittel *ine dritt'-el*
70	siebzig *seep'-sik*	$\frac{1}{2}$	ein Halb *ine hahlb*
80	achtzig *akt'-sik*	$\frac{3}{4}$	drei Viertel *dry feer'-tel*

TIME

today heute *hoyt'*-e
yesterday gestern *ges'-tern*
tomorrow morgen *mohr'-gen*
last year letztes Jahr *letst'-ess yahr*
next year nächstes Jahr *nayk'-stess yahr*
this morning dieser Morgen *deez-'er mohr'-gen*
this afternoon dieser Nachmittag *deez'-er nahk'-mit-tahg*
this evening dieser Abend *deez'-er ahb'-end*
tonight heute Abend *hoyt'*-e *ahb'-end*
last night gestern Nacht *ges'-tern nahkt*
tomorrow night morgen Abend *mohr'-gen ahb'-end*
next week nächste Woche *nayk'-ste vok'-e*
last week letze Woche *letst'-e vok'-e*
second Sekunde *f. seck-oonn'-de*
minute Minute *f. meen-oot'-e*
hour Stunde *f. shtoonn'-de*
day Tag *m. tahg*
fortnight vierzehn Tage *feer'-tsayn tahg'-e*
month Monat *m. moh'-naht*
early früh *frEE*
late spät *shpayt*
one o'clock ein Uhr *ine oor*
quarter past one viertel zwei *feert'-el tsvy*
half past one halb zwei *hahlp tsvy*
quarter to two dreiviertel zwei *dry'-feert-el tsvy*
two o'clock zwei Uhr *tsvy oor*
three o'clock drei Uhr *dry oor*
noon Mittag *mit'-tahg*
midnight Mitternacht *mit'-ter-nahkt*

Note how one says 'half to' the hour instead of 'half ast'. Also remember that the 24-hour clock method of otation is used in timetables and verbally in enquiry ffices or making appointments, etc. 1 p.m. = 13.00 hours dreizehn Uhr, *dry'-tsayn oor*), 2.30 p.m. = 14.30 (vierzehn hr dreissig, *feer'-tsayn oor dry'-sik*) and so on, expressing each pair of figures in the number individually, ith 'Uhr' in between.

COLOURS

lack schwarz *shvarts*	**brown** braun *brown*
hite weiss *vice*	**grey** grau *grow*
ed rot *roht*	**beige** beige *beige*
range orange *ohr-an'-she*	**pink** rosa *roh'-zah*
ellow gelb *gelp*	**mauve** lila *lee'-lah*
reen grün *grEEn*	**dark** dunkel *doonngk'-el*
lue blau *blow*	**light** hell *hel*

otels

German hotels and restaurants, which range from the 3th century inn to the ultra-modern de-luxe hotel, are quipped to meet the demands of the most discriminating isitor. Many were once castles belonging to barons and rincelings, and some inns boast of centuries of tradition during which they have catered for kings and emperors, famous artists and men of letters. There are many mountain hotels and châlets situated in the picturesque settings of the Bavarian Alps, the Black Forest, the Harz and other mountainous districts.

All offer high-class international fare as well as tasty local dishes such as chicken stew, eel soup, and many other fish dishes in the coastal areas. (See the section on "Food and Wine").

The price of hotel rooms, which vary according to category, are clearly marked for the convenience of visitors. Nowadays, most prices shown include bed, breakfast, service charge and taxes. Likewise, charges for meals, drinks, etc. include service charge and tax. There are no licensing hours for the serving of alcoholic drinks.

A list of hotels covering either the whole of West Germany or individual regions may be obtained from the German National Tourist Office, 61 Conduit Street, London W.1.

USEFUL WORDS AND PHRASES

ashtray Aschenbecher *m. ahsh'-en-bek-er*
basin Waschbecken *n. vahsh'-beck-en*
bath Badewanne *f. bah'-de-vahnn-e*
bathroom Badezimmer *n. bah'-de-tsim-er*
bed Bett *n. bet*
bedroom Schlafzimmer *n. shlahf'-tsim-er*
  (single —) Einzelzimmer *n. ine'-tsel-tsim-er*
  (double —) Doppelzimmer *n. dop'-el-tsim-er*
bill Rechnung *f. rek'-noonng*
blanket Bettdecke *f. bet'-deck-e*

30

board (full) Voll-Pension *f.* *foll'-pahng-se-ohn*
  (half —) Halb-Pension *f.* *hahlp'-pahng-se-ohn*
breakfast Frühstück *n.* *fr*EE*-sht*EE*-ck*
chair Stuhl *m.* *shtool*
chambermaid Zimmermädchen *n.* *tsim'-er-mait-ken*
coat-hanger Bügel *m.* *b*EE*'-gel*
dining-room Esszimmer *n.* *ess'-tsim-mer*
dinner Hauptmahlzeit *f.* *hawpt-'mahl-tsite*
eiderdown Daunendecke *f.* *down'-en-deck-*e
heating Heizung *f.* *hite'-tsoonngk*
hot-water bottle Wärmeflasche *f.* *vairm'-e-flahsh-*e
key Schlüssel *m.* *shl*EESS*'el*
lavatory Toilette *f.* *toy-lett'-*e
lift Fahrstuhl *m.* *fahr'-shtool,* Lift *m.* *lift*
lignt Licht *n.* *likt*
lounge Gesellschaftszimmer *n.* *ge-zell'-shahfts-tsim'-er*
lunch Mittagessen *n.* *mit'-tahg-ess-*en
manager Leiter, Vorsteher *m.* *lite'-er, fohr'-shtay-*er
mattress Matratze *f.* *maht-rahtt'-*se
message Botschaft *f* *boht'-shahft*
mirror Spiegel *m.* *shpeeg'-el*
page boy Hoteldiener *m.* *hoh-tel'-deen-er*
pillow Kissen *n.* *kiss'-*en
porter Träger *m.* *trayg'-er*
proprietor Besitzer *m.* *be-zit-ser*
reading lamp Leselampe *f.* *lay'-ze-lahmp-*e
receptionist Empfangspersonal *n.*, Emfangsdame, *f.*
             emp'-fahngs-pair-zohn-ahl,
             *emp'-fahngs-dahm-*e
sheet (Bett) Laken *n.* *(bet) lahk'-*en
shower Dusche *f.* *doosh'-*e

soap Seife *f. sy'-f*e
switch Schalter *m. shahlt'-er*
table Tisch *m. tish*
tap (Wasser) Hahn *m.* (*vahss'-er*) *hahn*
towel Handtuch *n. hahnnt'-took*
valet Diener *m. deen'-er*
wardrobe Kleiderschrank *m. kly'-der-shrahnk*
window Fenster *n. fenst'-er*

I am Mr (Mrs) . . .	Mein Name ist Herr (Frau) . . .
	mine nahm'-e ist hairr (frow)
Can I have a room for one night?	Kann ich ein Zimmer für eine Nacht haben?
	kahnn ik ine tsim'-er fEEr ine'-e nakt hah'-ben
I (We) wish to stay . . . days (one week, two weeks)	Ich will (Wir wollen) . . . Tage (eine Woche, zwei Wochen) bleiben
	ik vill (veer voll'-en) . . . tahg'-e (ine'-e vok'-e, tsvy vok'en) bly'ben
What are your terms?	Wie sind Ihre Bedingungen?
	vee zind eer'-e be-ding'-oong-en
May I see the room?	Kann ich mir das Zimmer ansehen?
	kahnn ik meer duss tsim'-er ahn'-zay-en
Any room will do	Mir ist jedes Zimmer recht
	meer ist yaid'-es tsim'-er rekt
It is too noisy	Es ist zu laut
	ess ist tsoo lowt

I want a room for myself only

Iche möchte ein Zimmer für mich allein haben

ik merk'-te ine tsim'-er fEEr mik ah-line' hah'-ben

Have you a room with a private bathroom?

Haben Sie ein Zimmer mit einem privaten Bade-zimmer?

hah'-ben zee ine tsim'-er mit ine'-em pree-vaht'-en bahd'-e-tsim-er

Can I overlook the sea (garden)?

Ich möchte Ausblick auf das Meer (den Garten)

ik merk'-te ows'-blik owf duss mayr (dayn gahr'-ten)

I require full board

Ich möchte Voll-Pension

ik merk'-te foll pahng-se-ohn'

I only require breakfast

Ich möchte nur Frühstück

ik merk'-te noor frEE'-shtEEk

May I have breakfast in my room?

Kann ich Frühstück auf meinem Zimmer haben?

kahnn ik frEE'-shtEEk owf mine'-em tsim'-er hah'-ben

I require breakfast and an evening meal

Ich möchte Frühstück und eine Abendmahlzeit haben

ik merk'-te frEE'-shtEEk oond ine'-e ah-bend'-mahl-tsite hah'-ben

Where is the bathroom?

Wo ist das Badezimmer?

voh ist duss bah'-de-tsim'-er

May I have that table?

Kann ich diesen Tisch haben?

kahnn ik deez'-en tish hah'-ben

May I dine now?

Kann ich meine Mahlzeit jetzt haben?

kahnn ik mine'-e mahl'-tsite yetst hah'-ben

C

33

May I dine earlier (later)?   Kann ich früher (später) die
Mahlzeit einnehmen?

kahnn ik *free'-er (shpayt'-er) dee mahl'-tsite ine'-nay-men*

May I have a packed meal?   Kann ich eine Mahlzeit
gepackt mitbekommen?

kahnn ik *ine'-e mahl'-tsite ge-pahkt' mit'-be-kom-men*

What time do you close?   Wann wird bei Ihnen
geschlossen?

vahnn veert by een'-en ge-shloss'-en

I shall be back at ...   Ich werde um ... zurück sein

ik vair'-de oomm ... tsoo-reek' zine

I am going to bed   Ich gehe jetzt ins Bett

ik gay-e yetst ins bet

Please call me at ...   Bitte wecken Sie mich um ...

bitt'-e veck'-en zee mik oom

Don't disturb me in the morning   Stören Sie mich bitte nicht
am Morgen

shter'-en zee mik bitt'-e nikt ahm mohr'-gen

Come in!   Herein!

hair-ine'

May I have a ... ?   Kann ich ein ... haben?

kahnn ik *ine ... hah'-ben*

Please open (close) the window   Machen Sie bitte das
Fenster auf (zu)

mak'-en zee bitt'-e duss fenst'-er owf (tsoo)

Are there any letters for me?   Ist irgendwelche Post für
mich gekommen?

ist eerg'-ent-velk-e posst feer mik ge-kom'-en

Can you do my laundry?   Können Sie mir meine
Wäsche waschen?

kern'-en zee meer mine'-e vesh'-e vahsh'-en

I need these clothes washed	Diese Sachen müssen gewaschen werden
deez'-e sahk'-en MEESS'-en ge-vahsh'-en ver'-den	
Can I have them back tomorrow?	Kann ich sie morgen zurück haben?
kahnn ik zee mohr'-gen tsoor-EEk' hah'-ben	
Would you repair that?	Könnten Sie mir das reparieren?
kern'-ten zee meer duss ray-pahr-eer'-en	
Can I have this pressed?	Könnte ich das geplättet haben?
kern'-te ik duss ge-plett'-et hah'-ben	
May I have my bill?	Könnte ich meine Rechnung haben?
kern'-te ik mine'-e rek'-noong hah'-ben	
Where is my luggage?	Wo ist mein Gepäck?
voh ist mine ge-peck'	
Would you get me a taxi?	Bitte rufen Sie mir eine Taxe
bitt'-e roof'-en zee meer ine'-e tahx'-e	

Camping and Caravanning

The Federal Republic has over 1,100 well-equipped camping sites, most of which are open from mid-May to the end of September, while in some winter sports areas you will find sites open all the year round. The German National Tourist Office, 61 Conduit Street, London W.1, will supply a map showing a selection of camping sites, and a more detailed guide can be purchased from the Deutscher Camping-Club, Mandlstr. 28, 8 Munich 23, West Germany.

More than 650 Youth Hostels are established throughout the country, some in ancient castles and others in modern buildings. There are also numerous mountain huts and shelters provided by hiking clubs, who also mark the more interesting trails. For a full list of German hostels, and a membership card, apply to the Y.H.A., 29 John Adam Street, London W.C.2, or to Deutsches Jugendherbergswerk, Bülowstr. 26, 493 Detmold, West Germany.

USEFUL WORDS AND PHRASES

boots Stiefel *m. shteef-*el
bridge Brücke *f. br*EE*k'-*e
bucket Eimer *m. i'-mer*
camp Lager *n. lah'-ger*
to camp lagern *lahg'-ern*
camping site Campingplatz *m. camping-plahtts*
cooking utensils Koch-Geräte *pl. kok'-ge-rayte*
cork-screw Korkzieher *m. kork'-tsee-er*
drinking water Trinkwasser *n. trink'-vahss-er*
east Osten *m. osst'-en*
farm Bauernhof *m. bow'-ern-hohf*
farmer Bauer *m. bow'-er*
field Feld *n. felt*

36

forest Wald *m. vahllt*
frying pan Bratpfanne *f. braht'-pfahnn-e*
ground sheet Grundtuch *n.*, Bodenlaken *n.*
        groont'-took, boh'-den-lahk-en
haversack Brotbeutel *m. broht'-boy-tel*
hike wandern *vahn'-dern*
hill Hügel *m. hee'-gel*
hitch hike wandern durch Wagen anhalten
        vahn'-dern doork vah'-gen ahn'-hahl-ten
ice Eis *n. ice*
inn Gasthaus *n. gahsst'-howss*
lake See *m. say*
log Scheit *n. shy't*
matches Streichhölzer *pl. shtryk'-herlt-ser*
mess-tin Kochgeschirr *n. kok'-ge-sheerr*
methylated spirit Brennspiritus *m. brenn'-shpeer-it-ooss*
mountain Berg *m. bairk*
mountain pass Gebirgspass *m. ge-beerrgs'-pahss*
north Norden *m. nord'-en*
paraffin Paraffin *n. pah'-raff-een*
path Fussweg *m. fooss'-vayg*
penknife Taschenmesser *n. tah'-shen-mess-er*
picnic Picknick *n. pic'-nic*
river Fluss *m. floohs*
road Strasse *f. shtrahss'-e.*
rope Strick *m. shtrick*
rubbish Kehricht *m.* Müll *m. kayr'-ikt,* MEEll
refuse bin Mülleimer *m.* MEEll'-ime-er
rucksack Rucksack *m. rook'-sahck*
saucepan Kochtopf *m. kok'-top'f*
shower Brause, *f.* Dusche *f. brow'-ze doosh'-e*

sleeping bag Schlafsack *m.* *schlaff'-sahck*
snow Schnee *m.* *shnay*
south Süden *m.* *SEED'-en*
storm Sturm *m.* *shtoorm*
stove Herd *m.* *hairt*
stream Bach *m.* *bahk*
summit Gipfel *m.* *ghip'-fel*
tent Zelt *n.* *tselt*
tent-peg Zelt-pflock *m.* *tselt'-pflock*
tent-pole Zelt-pfahl *m.* *tselt'-pfahl*
thermos Thermos (flasche) *f.* *tair'-moss (flahsh'-*e)
tin Dose *f.* *doh'-*ze
tin opener Dosenöffner *m.* *doh'-zen-erff-ner*
torch Taschenlampe *f.* *tahsh'-en-lahmp-*e
torch batteries Taschenlampenbatterien *pl.*
　　　　　　tahsh'en-lahmp-en-baht-e-ree-en
valley Tal *n.* *tahl*
village Dorf *n.* *dorf*
walk Spaziergang *m.* *shpaht-seer'-gahng*
waterfall Wasserfall *m.* *vahss'-er-fahll*
waterproof Regenmantel *m.* *ray'-ghen-mahnt-el*
waterproof (*adj.*) wasserdicht *vahss'-er-dikt*
weather (good, bad) (gutes, schlechtes) Wetter *n.*
　　　　　　　　(*goot'-*ess, *shlekt'-ess) vet'-er*
west Westen *m.* *vest'-en*
wind Wind *m.* *vinnt*
wood Holz *n.,* Wald *m.* *holts, vahlt*
youth hostel Jugendherberge *f.* *yoog'-ent-hair-bairg-*e

May I camp here?　　　　Kann ich hier lagern?
　　　kahnn i*k heer lahg'-ern*

Where is the nearest caravan site?	Wo ist der nächste Wohnwagenplatz?
voh ist der naykst'-e	*vohn'-vahg-en-plahtts*
What is the charge per night?	Was kostet es für eine Nacht?
vahss kost'-et ess fEER ine'-e nakt	
May we light a fire?	Dürfen wir ein Feure anmachen?
dEERf'-en veer ine foy'-er ahn'-mahk-en	
Where can I buy . . . ?	Wo kann ich . . . kaufen?
voh kahnn ik *. . . kowf'-en*	

Motoring

Travel is fast on German roads especially on the ever-expanding autobahn network, and if the motorist wishes to discover the real Germany he should use the by-ways rather than the highways.

British tourists visiting Germany with their own cars or motor cycles require only their driving licence and registration papers. All motor vehicles in West Germany are subject to compulsory third party insurance. Travellers arriving without the international green insurance card are able to arrange their third party cover at the frontier. No customs papers are required for vehicles not used for commercial purposes, or for trailers. It is advisable when travelling with a caravan or luggage trailer to carry an inventory in triplicate of all fittings and contents of particular value. This may be stamped by the German Customs at the frontier. The use of the vehicle by people permanently resident in Germany is not permitted.

Petrol and oil are in unlimited supply in the Federal Republic. Foreign vehicles entering West Germany during the tourist season and at weekends may enter with full tanks free of duty.

N.B. For travel to West Berlin all foreign nationals require a passport. Motorists must obtain a transit visa which will be issued at the control points on the East German frontier. It is unnecessary to apply in advance. For entry into East Germany or East Berlin motorists must have a visa which they can obtain from the German DEMOCRATIC Republic Consulate in their own country. Alternatively the entry visa may be applied for from the Deutsches Reisebüro, Zentrale Leitung, Friedrichstrasse 110/112, Berlin N4, which is the East German part of the city.

Rule of the road, Parking

Drive on the right, overtake on the left. On roads which have two lanes in each direction, you may remain in the left-hand (overtaking) lane if there is dense traffic on your right. But when columns have formed in both lanes, you are allowed to drive faster in the right-hand lane; if you happen to be in the left-hand lane you may move to the right only in order to turn off, stop, or follow directional arrows. Proper lane discipline is important.

Stopping becomes parking if you leave your car or stop for over three minutes. There is no longer a "No Parking" sign; if the international ones for "No Waiting" and "No Stopping" (Clearway) are not posted, remember not to park too close to junctions, traffic lights, in narrow roads or facing oncoming traffic.

Precedence

Traffic coming from the right has priority at crossroads and junctions wherever there is no priority sign or traffic light, unless entering the main road from a car park, service station, private road, path or forest track. Your right of way is signalled by a yellow diamond or the more familiar thick arrow inside a red triangle. The former gives you priority for some distance ahead, while the latter is good for the next intersection only. The usual international sign, an inverted red triangle, denotes that you must give way.

Speed limits

In built-up areas a limit of 50 km/h (31 mph) is shown by the town's name on a yellow plate. The same plate, with a red diagonal stripe, marks the end of both limit and area. On roads outside built-up areas, except autobahns, dual carriageways and those with at least two marked lanes in each direction, there is now a speed limit of 100 km/h (62 mph) for all vehicles under 2.8 tons weight. Heavier vehicles—lorries, buses, cars towing caravans or trailers—are restricted to 80 km/h (50 mph) on *all* roads and autobahns. If a special speed limit is applied to a stretch of road, the usual signs will advise you.

Automobile Clubs

The ADAC (11a Königinstrasse, 8 Munich 22), the AvD (16 Lyoner Strasse, 6 Frankfurt-Niederrad), and the DTC (30 Elisabeth Strasse, 8 Munich 13) have offices in many German towns and in West Berlin. They will gladly assist foreign motorists; the ADAC and AvD run road patrols on the autobahns and major arterial routes, and these are always at your disposal if you require assistance. Ask for "Strassenwachthilfe" on the roadside emergency telephone.

Translation of some common road signs

Achtung! Baustelle
Caution! Construction

Achtung! Strassenbahn
Caution! Tramway

Bauarbeiten
Men working

Bei Frost Glatteisgefahr
Icy in cold weather

Ende der Autobahn
End of autobahn

Fahrbahnwechsel
Change lane

Freie Fahrt
No speed limit

Feldbahn, Bahnübergang
Level crossing

Frostaufbrüche
Frost damage

Frostschäden
Frost damage

Gefährliche Einmündung
Dangerous junction

Gefährliche Kurve
Dangerous curve

Gegenverkehr
Two-way traffic

Gegenverkehr hat Vorfahrt
Oncoming traffic has right of way

Gesperrt für Fahrzeuge aller Art
Closed to all vehicles

Glatteis
Ice

Höchstgeschwindigkeit
Limit speed

Jetzt umschalten
Change gear

Langsam fahren
Drive slowly

Nicht überholen
No overtaking

Nur für Anlieger
Entry to adjacent premises only

Radweg kreuzt
Cycle track crossing

Rasthaus
Rest house

Schlechte Fahrbahn
Bad road

Schlechte Wegstrecke
Bad road

Starkes Gefälle
Steep gradient

Steinschlag
Fallen rock

Überholen verboten
Overtaking prohibited

Unebenheiten
Rough road

Verengte Fahrbahn
Road narrows

Vorsicht beim Überholen
Overtake with caution

USEFUL WORDS AND PHRASES

accelerator Gaspedal *n. gahs'-pay-dahl*
air pump Luftpumpe *f. loofft'-poomp-*e
back axle Rückachse *f.* rEEk'*-ahk-s*e
battery Batterie *f. bahtt'-er-ee*
big end Pleuellager *n. ploy-'ell-ahg-er*
body Karosserie *f. kahr-oss-er-ee'*
bolt Schraube *f. shrowb'-*e
bonnet Haube *f. howb'-*e

boot Gepäckraum *m.* *ge-peck'-rowm*
brake Bremse *f.* *brem'-ze*
  (hand —) Hand-Bremse *f.* *hahnnt'-brem-ze*
brake lining Bremsbelag *m.* *brems'-bel-ahg*
breakdown Panne *f.* *pahnn'-e*
breakdown van Abschleppwagen *m.* *ahp-shlepp-vahg'-en*
bumper Stossstange *f.* *shtohss'-shtahn-ge*
camshaft Nockenwelle *f.* *nock'en-vell'-e*
car Auto *n.*, Wagen *m.* *ow'-toh, vahg'-en*
caravan Wohnwagen *m.* *vohn'-vahg-en*
carburettor Vergaser *m.* *fair-gahz-'er*
choke Luftklappe *f.* *looft'-klahpp-e*
clutch Kupplung *f.* *koopp'-loong*
distributor Zündverteiler *m.* *tsEEnd-'fair-tile-er*
door Tür *f.* *tEEr*
drive (v) fahren *fahr'-en*
driver Fahrer *m.* *fahr'-er*
engine Motor *m.* *moh'-tohr*
exhaust Auspuff *m.* *ows'-pooff*
fan Ventilator *m.* *vain-tee-laht'-ohr*
fan belt Keilriemen *m.* *kile'-reem-en*
funnel Trichter *m.* *trik'-ter*
garage Garage *f.* *gah-rahsh'-e*
gear Gang *m.* *ganng*
gear box Getriebekasten *m.* *ge-treeb'-er-kahsst-en*
gear lever Gangschaltung *f.* *gahng'-shahlt-oong*
(starting) handle Anlassknobel *m.* *ahn'-lahss-k'nohb-el*
(door) handle (Tür) Griff *m.* *(tEEr) grif*
highway code Verkehrsregeln *pl.* *fair-kairs'-ray-gheln*
hood Verdeck *n.* *fair-deck'*
horn Hupe *f.* *hoop'-e*

45

hub cap Radkappe *f.* *raht'-kahpp*-e
ignition Zündung *f.* *tsEEnd'-oong*
indicator Blinker *m.* *blink*-er
inner tube Innenschlauch *m.* *inn'-en-shlowk*
jack Wagenwinde *f.* *vah'-gen-vinn'-d*e
lever (n.) Bremshebel *m.* *brems'-hayb'-el*
licence Führerschein *m.* *fEEr'-er-shin*e
lights (head) Scheinwerferlampen *shine-'vair-fer-lahmp-en*
lights (side) Seitenlampen *sy'-ten-lahmp-en*
lights (rear) Schlusslichter *shloos'-lik-ter*
lorry Lastwagen *m.* *lahst'-vah-gen*
lubrication Schmiersystem *n.* *shmeer'-seest-aim*
mechanic Autoschlosser *m.* *ow'-toh-shloss-er*
mirror Spiegel *m.* *shpeeg'-el*
motorway Autobahn *f.* *ow'-toh-bahn*
number plate Nummernschild *n.* *noomm'-er-shilt*
nut Schraubenmutter *f.* *shrowb-en-moott'-er*
oil Öl *n.* *erl*
pedestrian Fussgänger *m.* *fooss'-geng-er*
petrol Benzin *n.* *bent-seen'*
petrol pump Benzin Pumpe *n.* *bent-seen' poomp'*-e
petrol station Tankstelle *f.* *tahnk'-shtel-l*e
piston Kolben *m.* *kolb'-en*
piston ring Kolbenring *m.* *kolb'-en-ring*
plug Zündkerze *f.* *tsEEnd'-kairts*-e
propeller shaft Antriebswelle *f.* *ahnt'-reeps-vell'*-e
radiator Kühler *m.* *kEEl'*-er
rim Felge *f.* *felg'*-e
saloon limousine *f.* *lee-moo-seen'*-e
screw Schraube *f.* *shrowb'*-e
screwdriver Schraubenzieher *m.* *shrowb-en-tsee'*-er

shock absorber Stossdämpfer *m. shtohss'-damf-er*

skid (v. and n.) schleudern, Schleudern *n. shloyd'-ern*

spanner Schraubenschlüssel *m. shrowb'-en-shlEESS-el*

spares Ersatzteile *pl. air-sahts-'tile-e*

speed Geschwindigkeit *f. ge-shvind'-ig-kite*

speed limit erlaubte Höchstgeschwindigkeit *f.*
　　　　　air-lowp'-te herkste-ge-shvind'-ig-kite

speedometer Geschwindigkeitsmesser *m.*
　　　　　ge-shvind'-ig-kites-mess-er

spring Sprungfeder *f. shproong'-fayd-er*

starter Anlasser *m. ahn'-lahss-er*

steering wheel Steuerrad *n. shtay'-er-rahd*

tank Benzintank *m. bent-seen'-tahnk*

traffic (Strassen) Verkehr *m. (shtrahss'-en) fair-kair'*

traffic lights Verkehrsampeln *pl. fair-kairs'-ahmp-eln*

trailer Anhängerwagen *m. ahn'-haing-er-vah-gen*

transmission Kraftübertragung *f.*
　　　　　krahft'-EE-ber-trahg-oong

two-stroke mixture Zweitakt-Mischung *f.*
　　　　　tsvy'-tahkt-mish'-oong

tyre Reifen *m. rife'-en*

(tubeless —) schlauchloser — *shlowk'-lohs-er —*

valve Schlauchventil *n. shlowk'-ven-teel'*

vehicle Fahrzeug *n. fahr'-tsoyg*

washer Dichtungsring *m. dikt'-oongs-ring*

wheel Rad *n. raht*

　　(back —) Hinter— *hint'-er—*

　　(front —) Vorder— *ford'-er—*

　　(spare —) Ersatz— *air-sahts'—*

window Fenster *n.* *fenst'-er*
  (rear —) Heck— *heck'*—
  (side —) Seiten— *site'-en*—
windscreen Windschutzscheibe *f.* *vint'-shoots-shybe-*e
windscreen wiper Scheibenwischer *m.* *shyb'-en-vish-er*
wing Kotflügel *m.* *koht'-fl*EEg*-el*

I want some petrol (oil, water)	Ich brauche etwas Benzin (Öl, Wasser)

    *ik browk'-*e *et'-vahs bent-seen' (*e*rl, vahss'-er)*

Would you check the oil?	Bitte prüfen Sie das Öl

    *bitte'-*e *pr*EEf*'-en see duss e*rl

Would you check the tyre pressures?	Bitte prüfen Sie den Reifen-Druck

    *bitt'-*e *pr*EEf*'-en see dain ry'-fen-drook*

Do you do repairs?	Machen Sie Reparaturen?

    mahk'-en see rep-ah-raht-oor'-en

Can you repair my . . .?	Können Sie mein . . . reparieren?

    kernn'-en see mine . . . rep-ah-reer'-en

How long will it take?	Wielange wird es dauern?

    *vee-lahng'-*e *ve*e*rt ess dow'-ern*

I have run out of petrol	Ich habe kein Benzin mehr

    *ik hahb'-*e *kine bent-seen' mair*

The engine is overheating	Der Motor ist überhitzt

    der moh'-tohr ist EE*-ber-hitst'*

May I park here?	Kann ich hier parken?

    kahnn ik heer pahrk'-en

Where may I park?	Wo kann ich parken?

    voh kahnn i*k pahrk'-en*

How far is it to . . . ?	Wie weit ist es nach . . . ?

vee vite ist ess nahk . . .

How far is the next garage (filling station)?	Wie weit ist es bis zur nächsten Garage (Tankstelle)?

vee vite ist ess bis tsoor nayk'-sten gah-rahsh'-e (tahnk'-shtell-e)

What time does the garage (filling station) close?	Wann wird die Garage (Tankstelle) geschllossen?

vahnn veert de gah-rahsh'-e (tahnk'-shtell-e) ge-shloss'-en

My brakes are slipping (binding)	Meine Bremsen sind zu lose (zu fest)

mine'-e brem'-zen sinnt tsoo loh'-ze (tsoo fest)

May I wash my hands?	Kann ich mir meine Hände waschen?

kahnn ik meer mine'-e hend-e vahsh'-en

May I use your telephone?	Kann ich Ihr Telefon benutzen?

kahnn ik eer tay-le-fohn' ben-oots'-en

I want a new fan belt	Ich brauche einen neuen Keilriemen

ik browk'-e ine'-en noy'-en kile-reem'-en

The clutch is slipping	Die Kupplung rutscht

de koopl'-oong rootsht

Is this the road to . . . ?	Ist dies die Strasse nach . . . ?

ist dees de shtrahss'-e nahk . . .

Would you wipe the windscreen?	Können Sie bitte meine Windschutzscheibe waschen?

kernn'-en see bitt'-e mine'-e vint'-shoots-shybe-e vahsh'-en

D

49

Could you clean it right away?	Könnten Sie es gleich säubern?
	kernnt'-en see ess gly'k soyb'-ern
May I park without lights?	Kann ich meinen Wagen hier ohne Licht parken?
kahnn ik mine'-en vah'-gen heer ohn'-e likt pahr'-ken	
I want to hire a car for . . .	Ich möchte einen Wagen nach . . . mieten
ik merk'-te ine'-en vah'-gen nahk . . . meet'-en	
Would you fit a new bulb?	Können Sie mir bitte eine neue Birne einsetzen?
kernn'-en see meer bitt'-e ine'-e noy'-e beern'-e ine'-sets-en	
Would you mend this puncture?	Können Sie mir bitte diese Radpanne reparieren?
kernn'-en see meer bitt'-e deez'-e rahd'-pahnn-e rep-ah-reer'-en	
May I borrow . . . ?	Kann ich . . . borgen?
kahnn ik . . . bohrg'-en	

Public Transport

BY RAIL

The German Federal Railways, one of the first railway systems in the world, are outstanding for their punctuality and general efficiency, whether you want a good night's rest en route, a substantial meal in the dining car, or just a comfortable journey.

Many fare reductions are available; return journeys over 50 km, round-trip and "runabout" tickets, group travel, children under ten (four-year-olds travel free), and so on. A supplementary charge, called a "Zuschlag", is made for travel on Inter-City trains and the Trans European Express (TEE). If you buy a ticket in Germany and take a "D" train for a journey of under 50 km., you will have to pay a smaller supplement. Seat reservations cost a little extra, and luggage can be registered to your destination. Holders of international tickets may break their journey at any point; stopping trains are marked "Personenzug". There are car/sleeper services for those who prefer to avoid long and tiring road travel (details will be supplied by the DER Travel Service, 16 Orchard Street, London W.1.).

Some rail tickets can be used on the Rhine and Moselle cruise vessels. When you transfer from train to boat you will pay a supplementary charge based on the type of ticket held and the distance you wish to travel on the river.

USEFUL WORDS AND PHRASES

air Luft *f. loofft*
airless zu wenig Luft *tsoo vay'-nik loofft*
alight aussteigen *ows'-shty-gen*
attendant Dienstpflichtiger *m.* Wärter *m.*
            deenst'-flikt-tee-ger, vairt'-er
booking office Fahrkarten-Schalter *m.*
            fahr'-kart-en-shahlt-er

carriage Abteil *n.* Wagen *m.* *ahp-tile', vah'-gen*
case Koffer *m.* *koff-er*
compartment Abteilung *f.* *ahp-tile'-oong*
corridor Korridor *m.* *korr'-ee-dohr*
dining-car Speisewagen *m.* *shpy'-ze-vah-gen*
enquiry office Auskunftsbüro *n.* *owss'-koonfts-bEEr-oh*
entrance Eingang *m.* *ine'-gahng*
exit Ausgang *m.* *owss'-gahng*
guard Schaffner *m.* *shahff'-ner*
luggage rack Gepäcknetz *n.* *ge-peck'-nets*
luggage van Gepäckwagen *m.* *ge-peck'-vah-gen*
platform Bahnsteig *m.* *bahn'shty'k*
seat Platz *m.* Sitz *m.* *plahts, sits*
seat reservation Platzkarten-Bestellung *f.*
                 plahts'-kahr-ten-be-shtell'-oong
sleeping berth Schlafwagenbett *n.* *shlahf'-vah-gen-bet*
station Bahnhof *m.* *bahn'-hohf*
station master Bahnhofsvorsteher *m.*
                 bahn'-hofs-fohr-shtay-er
ticket (single) Fahrkarte *f.* *fahr'-kart-e*
  (return) Rückfahrkarte *f.* *rEEk'-fahr-kart-e*
ticket collector Fahrkartenkontrolleur *m.*
                 fahr'-kart-en-kon-troll-er
timetable Fahrplan *m.* *fahr'-plahn*
train Zug *m.* *tsook*
waiting room Wartezimmer *n.* *vahrt'-e-tsim-er*
window Fenster *n.* *fenst'-er*

I want a single (return)	Ich möchte eine Fahrkarte
ticket to . . .	(Rückfahrkarte) nach . . .

ik merk'-te ine'-e fahr'-kart-e (rEEk'-fahr-kart-e) nack

I have a reserved seat	Ich habe einen Platz reserviert

ik hahb'-e ine'-en plahts ray-zairv-eert'

Please find me a seat	Bitte suchen Sie mir einen Platz

bitt'-e sook'-en see meer ine'-en plahts

I would like a smoking (non-smoking) compartment	Ich möchte ein Raucher (Nicht-Raucher) Abteil

ik merk'-te ine rowk'-er (nikt'-rowk-er) ahp-tile'

Could I have a window seat?	Kann ich einen Fensterplatz haben?

kahnn ik ine'-en fenst'-er-plahts hahb'-en

This seat is reserved	Dieser Platz ist reserviert

deez'-er plahts ist ray-zairv-eert'

That seat is taken	Jener Platz ist besetzt

yain'-er plahts ist be-zettst'

Are there any first class seats?	Gibt es irgendwelche erster-Klasse-Plätze?

gibt ess eerg'-ent-velk-e airst'-er klahss-e-pletts'-e

Could you find me a berth?	Können Sie mir einen Schlafwagenplatz besorgen?

kern'-nen see meer ine'-en shlahff'-vah-gen-plahts be-zohrg'-en

May I open (close) the window?	Darf ich das Fenster auf-machen (schliessen)?

darhf ik duss fenst'-er owf'-mahk-en (shleess'-en)

How long do we stop here?	Wielange haben wir hier Aufenthalt?

vee lahng'-e hahb'-en veer heer owf'-en-tahlt

Where is the inspector?	Wo ist der Aufseher?

voh ist der owf'-zay-er

Please mind my seat   Bitte passen Sie auf meinen
                            Platz auf
    bitt'-e pahss'-en see owf mine'-en plahts owf

Which way is the dining car?   Wo ist der Speisewagen?
    voh ist der shpyz'-e-vah-gen

What time is lunch (dinner)?   Wann gibt es Mittagessen
                                     (Abendessen)?
    vahnn gibt ess mitt'-ahg-ess-en (ahb'-end-ess-en)

Porter, take this luggage to   Träger, bringen Sie bitte
the left-luggage office   das Gepäck zur
                                     Gepäckaufbewahrungsstelle
    trayg'-er, bring'-en see bitt'-e duss ge-peck' tsoor
    ge-peck'-owf-be-vahr-oongs-shtell-e

Would you get me a taxi   Können Sie mir bitte ein
to . . . Hotel?   Auto für . . Hotel besorgen?
    kernn'-en see meer bitt'-e ine ow'-toh
    fEEr . . . hoht-ell' be-zourg'-en

Where is the booking   Wo ist der
office (enquiry office)? Fahrkartenschalter
                             (das Auskunftsbüro)?
    voh ist der fahr'-kahrt-'en-shahlt-er
    (duss ows'-koonfts-bEE-roh)

What time does the train   Wann geht der Zug nach . . .
leave for . . . ?   . . . ab?
    vahnn gayt der tsook nahk . . . ahp

Which platform, please?   Welcher Bahnsteig?
    velk-er bahn'-shty'k

Is this the right train   Ist das der richtige Zug
for . . . ?   nach . . . ?
    ist duss der rikt'-ee-ge tsook nahk . . .

Does it go direct?	Geht er direkt?
	gayt air dee-rekt'
Must I change?	Muss ich umsteigen?
	mooss ik oom'-shty-gen
Where do I change?	Wo muss ich umsteigen?
	voh mooss ik oom'-shty-gen
What time is the first	Wann geht der erste
(next, last) train for . . . ?	(nächste, letzte) Zug
	nach . . . ?
vahnn gayt der airst'-e (naykst'-e, letst'-e) tsook nahk	
Where is the nearest hotel?	Wo ist das nächste Hotel?
	voh ist duss naykst'-e hoh-tell'

BY COACH OR RIVER STEAMER

Bus and coach services are run by the German Federal Railways, the German Federal Posts, the German Touring Association, and numerous private agencies. Federal Railway coaches are painted red, and Federal Posts are yellow.

River and lake services. A more leisurely way of approaching and travelling about Germany is by boat on lake and river.

Between Easter and October passenger boats of the "Köln – Düsseldorfer Rheindampfschiffahrt" and other companies ply on the Rhine; you can travel from Rotterdam to Basle by cabin-class steamer. During the summer there are regular services on the rivers Weser, Moselle, Lahn, Fulda, Ruhr, Main, Neckar and Danube, and on the lower reaches of the Elbe. The seasonal boat traffic on

Lake Constance is almost unlimited, and regular services operate on the Bavarian lakes and on numerous lakes and reservoirs in the uplands, and on the Berlin lakes.

Mountain railways and cabin cable cars are plentiful in the upland and Alpine regions – as well as many chair- and ski-lifts. These allow easy and comfortable access to the mountain tops, so ensuring that practically no corner of the country is inaccessible.

USEFUL WORDS AND PHRASES

airport Flughafen *m. flook'-hahf-en*
alight aussteigen *ows'-shtyg-en*
berth Koje *f. koh'-ye*
board *v.* einsteigen *ine'-shtyg-en*
boot Gepäckraum *m. ge-peck'-rowm*
bus Autobus *m. ow'-toh-booss*
canal Kanal *m. kahn-ahl'*
coach Autobus *m. ow'-toh-booss*
conductor Schaffner *m. shahffn'-er*
connection Verbindung *f. fair-binn'-doong*
deck Deck *n. deck*
downstream stromabwärts *strohm-ahp'-vairts*
draught (air) Zug *m. tsook*
driver Führer *m. fEER'-er*
embark einschiffen *ine'-shif-en*
express boat Schnelldampfer *m. shnell'-dahm-fer*
fare Fahrpreis *m. fahr'-price*
ferry *n.* Fähre *f. fay'-re*
land *v.* landen *lahnd'-en*

56

motor launch Motorboot *n. moh'-tohr-boht*
observation lounge Aussichtssaal *m. ows'-sikts-sahl*
passenger Passagier *m. pahss-ah-sheer'*
port Hafen *m. hahf'-en*
quay Kai *m. ky*
river Fluss *m. floos*
river bank Ufer *n. oof-er*
ship Schiff *n. shiff*
steamer Dampfer *m. dahm'-fer*
steward Steward *m. shtoo'-ahrt*
sun-deck Sonnendeck *f. son'-en-deck*
upstream stromaufwärts *strohm-owf'-vairts*
voyage Reise *f. ry'-ze*

Where is the coach station?	Wo ist die Autobus-Haltestelle?
	voh ist de ow'-toh-booss-hahl'-te-shtell-e
What time do you leave (arrive)?	Wann fahren (kommen) Sie an?
	vahnn fahr'-en (kom'-en) see ahn
I want to get off at . . .	Ich möchte bei . . . aussteigen
	ik merkt'-e by . . . ows'-shty-gen
Will you tell me when we arrive?	Wollen Sie mir sagen, wann wir ankommen?
	voll'-en see meer sahg'-en, vahnn veer ahn'-kom-en·
Do you pass . . . ?	Kommen Sie bei . . . vorbei?
	kom'-en see by . . . for-by'

Do you go near . . . ?	Kommen Sie in die Nähe von . . . ?
	kom'-en see in de nay'-e fon
Will you put this in the boot (on the roof)?	Wollen Sie das in den Gepäckraum (aufs Verdeck) legen?
	voll'-en see duss in dayn ge-peck'-rowm (owfs fair-deck') lay'-gen
There is a draught	Hier ziet es
	heer tseet ess
Would you please open (close) the window?	Würden Sie bitte das Fenster öffnen (schliessen)?
	veerd'-en see bitt'-e duss fenst'-er erff'-nen (shleess'-en)
May I put this on the rack?	Kann ich das auf das Gepäcknetz tun?
	kahnn ik duss owf duss ge-peck'-nets toon
Do you return from here?	Kommen Sie von hier zurück?
	kom'-en see fon heer tsoo-rEEk'
Do you start from here?	Fahren Sie von hier ab?
	fahr'-en see fon heer ahp

BY AIR

Deutsche Lufthansa and many other companies operate air services connecting West Germany with all parts of the world. Modern airports are available at West Berlin, Bremen, Cologne/Bonn, Düsseldorf, Frankfurt (Main), Hamburg, Hanover, Munich, Nuremberg (Nürnberg) and Stuttgart.

USEFUL WORDS AND PHRASES

air hostess Stewardess *f.* *shtoo-ahr-dess'*
airline Luftverkehrslinie *f.* *looft'-fair-kairs-leen-ye*
airport Flughafen *m.* *flook'-hahf-en*
case Koffer *m.* *koff'-er*
cloudy wolkig *vollk'-ik*
control tower Kontrollturm *m.* *kont-rol'-toorm*
crew Belegschaft *f.* *bel-aig'-shahft*
fog Nebel *m.* *nayb'-el*
jet aircraft Düsenflugzeug *n.* *dEEz'-en-flook-tsyog*
land landen, ankommen *lahnd'-en, ahn'-kom-en*
pilot Pilot *m.* *peel-oht'*
propellor Propeller *m.* *prohp-ell'-er*
rack Gepäcknetz *n.* *ge-peck'-nets*
route Strecke *f.* *shtreck'-e*
runway Rollbahn *f.* *roll'-bahn*
seat Platz *m.*, Sitz *m.* *plahts, sits*
seat belt Sicherheitsgurt *m.* *sik'-er-hites-goort*
steward Steward *m.* *shtoo'-ahrt*
take-off abfliegen *ahp'-fleeg-en*
window Fenster *n.* *fenst'-er*
wing Flügel *m.* *flEEg'-el*

When can I get a plane for . . . ?	Wann kann ich ein Flugzeug nach . . . bestellen?
	vahnn kahnn ik ine flook'-tsoyg nahk . . . be-shtell'-en
What time does it leave (arrive)?	Wann geht es ab? (Wann kommt es an?)
	vahnn gayt ess ahp (vahnn komt ess ahn)

Where does it touch down? Wo landet es?
voh lahnd'-et ess

Will you fasten (unfasten) Bitte machen Sie meinen
my seat belt? Sicherheitsgurt fest (ab)
bitt'-e mak'-en see mine'-en sik'-er-hites-goort fest (ahp)

Have you a map of the Haben Sie eine Landkarte
route? von der Strecke?
hahb'-en see ine'-e lahnd'-kahrt-e fon dair shtreck'-e

Will you adjust my seat? Würden Sie bitte meinen
Sitz regulieren?
VEErd'-en see meer bitt'-e mine'-en sits ray-goo-leer'-en

What is the weather report? Wie ist die Wettervoraus-
sage?
vee ist de vett'-er-for-ows-sahgh-e

May I have some cigarettes Kann ich Zigaretten
(brandy)? (Kognak) haben?
kahnn ik tsee-gah-ret'-en (kon'-yahk) hahb'-en

Where is that? Wo ist das?
voh ist duss

Are we on time? Sind wir pünktlich?
sint veer PEEnkt'-lik

Would you adjust the air Würden Sie bitte die
conditioner? Luftzufuhr regulieren?
VEErd'-en see bitt'-e de looft'-tsoo-foohr ray-goo-leer'-en

It is very hot Es ist sehr heiss
ess ist sair hice

I do not feel well Ich fühle mich nicht wohl
ik fEEl'-e mik nikt vohl

Food and Wine

Wherever you eat in Germany, the food is both tasty and abundant. Contrary to popular belief, the German meal does not consist solely of sauerkraut with pig's knuckles and gallons of beer. Vegetables and salads feature prominently in German cooking (the former often prepared in a way that disguises their plainness). Meat is usually cut up and cooked with other things, but the ordinary roast joint is more common than it once was. Lamb is still scarce. Baking is the German cook's strong point; cakes, fruit tarts, etc. are excellent.

Breakfast is typically continental in most hotels, consisting of coffee with buttered rolls and jam. The main meal of the day runs to three courses; the set menu is called "Tages-Gedeck".

In **North Germany** you will find the diet especially rich, and apart from local dishes such as chicken stew and roast goose, eel soup and eels both smoked and boiled, the following specialities are well worth trying.

Labskaus; a traditional sailors' dish consisting of cured pork, mashed potatoes, and sometimes herrings, served with poached egg and cucumber.

Rundstück Warm; a slice of bread or a roll covered with hot pork and gravy. This is a speciality of Hamburg.

Braunkohl mit Pinkel; popular in Bremen and Oldenburg, this consists of kale with cured pork chops, smoked bacon, smoked sausage and sausage with groats, served with roast potatoes.

Hamburg's *Aalsuppe* (eel soup) is very rich and is made of eels, beef and different extras including dumplings – very suitable for cold days.

Schnitzel Holstein; a veal or pork cutlet, topped by a fried egg with assorted vegetables.

Pannfisch is a mixture of fried fish and roast potatoes, and *Heideschnuckenbraten* (a speciality of the Lüneburg Heath) is based on roast lamb. Try also the cottage hams and sausages, *Knüppelkuchen,* butter cake, and *Bremer Klaben;* this is the Bremen version of those loaves of sweet bread (called *Klöben* in Holstein) containing raisins, candied peel and various spices – more like a Christmas cake than bread.

Among the hard liquors produced in North Germany are *Aquavit* (Flensburg), *Doornkaat* and *Seehund* (Norden, East Friesland), and *Ratzeputz* (Lüneburg Heath). Jamaica rum with hot water and sugar is popular throughout the region, and from Hannover comes *Lütje Lage* (a glass of beer and a glass of corn brandy). Beer, of course, can be found everywhere, and is best if cool.

From **central Germany** come the original Frankfurter sausages, *Sauerbraten* (beef pickled in vinegar and then roasted), and *Kasseler Rippenspeer.* This is cured and smoked pork chops; any item on the menu that contains the word "Kassel . . . " is a pork dish. Pork chops with *Sauerkraut* are popular, and the smoked ham from Westphalia is delectable – it is often served with *Pumpernickel,* the black rye bread found all over the country. The Harz district is renowned for its trout and for liqueurs distilled from fine herbs.

In Hesse you will find the splendid *Rheingau* wine and excellent cider. From the Rhine and Moselle valleys come those wines that are world-famous and, for those who prefer harder liquor there is *Münsterland Korn* (a rye whisky) and *Steinhäger* (gin). The beer brewed in Dortmund is among the finest in Germany.

Nowhere does the hospitality exceed that shown to the visitor to **Bavaria,** and typical of this region are the large beer cellars and garden restaurants where brass bands entertain the patrons. Traditional dishes are *Schlachtschüssel* (sausages with choice pieces of pork), pigs' knuckles with sauerkraut, *Spätzle* and the many other varieties of noodle dishes, dumplings, *Schmarrn* (pancakes), and an infinite variety of sausages. Try also the cheese from the Allgäu alps, and the delicious Nuremberg gingerbread (which is equally good in Aachen, on the Dutch frontier). Strong beers such as *Märzen, Bock* and *Salvator* are often accompanied by radishes, and the Franconian wines (as good as any from the Rhine) come in special green bottles known as *Bocksbeutel*. Mention must also be made of the brandies (cherry, raspberry) from the Black Forest.

The Wine Label

Many local wines that do not pretend to be of the finest quality are probably as good as the more well-known names, and many visitors are content to drink these. If, however, you want to sample a more varied selection of German wines, the label on the bottle can tell you a lot.

To start with it names the district and the vineyard, often followed by the type of vine. Riesling vines grow in the Rheingau, just downstream from Mainz; Sylvaner vines are from the opposite (left) bank of the Rhine, upstream from Mainz. These are the two most important types, and are of course found elsewhere in the country.

Not all grapes are picked at the same time; some are left until they are over-ripe, or until they look like raisins. Such special harvestings are mentioned on the label: *Trockenbeerenauslese* means that the wine is made from specially selected single grapes that have been left on the vine so long that they have shrivelled; *Beerenauslese* denotes an equally choice selection, but from slightly less aged fruit; *Auslese* is applied to wine made from selected over-ripe bunches, and *Spätlese* merely indicates that the grapes were late-harvested.

USEFUL WORDS FOR THE RESTAURANT

GENERAL

bar Bar *f.*, Ausschank *m.* *bahr, ows'-shahnk*
bill Rechnung *f.* *rek'-noong*
bottle Flasche *f.* *flahsh'-e*
cup Tasse *f.* *tahss'-e*
drink Getränk *n.* *ge-trenk'*
egg cup Eierbecher *m.* *i'-er-bek-er*
fork Gabel *f.* *gah'-bel*
glass Glas *n.* *glahss*
knife Messer *n.* *mess'-er*
menu Speisekarte *f.* *shpy'-ze-kahr-te*
plate Teller *m.* *tell'-er*
serviette Serviette *f.*, Mundtuch *f.*
       sair-vee-ett'-e, moont'-took

spoon Löffel *m. lerff'-el*
table Tisch *m. tish*
tip Trinkgeld *n. trink'-geld*
waiter Kellner *m. kell'-ner*
waitress Kellnerin *f. kell'-ner-in*
wine list Weinliste *f. vine'-list-*e

FOOD

apple Apfel *m. ahp'-f*el
banana Banane *f. bah-nahn'-*e
beans Bohnen *pl. bohn'-en*
beef Rindfleisch *n. rindt'-fly'sh*
biscuit Keks *m.* Zwieback *m. kayks, tsvee'-bahk*
bread Brot *n. broht*
butter Butter *f. boott'-e*r
cabbage Kohl *m. kohl*
cake Kuchen *m. kook'-en*
carrots Mohrrüben *pl. moh'-*rEEb-*en*
cauliflower Blumenkohl *m. bloo'-men-kohl*
cheese Käse *m. kays'-*e
chops Kotelettes *pl. kot-letts'*
cream Sahne *f. sahn'-*e
egg Ei *n. i*
fish Fisch *m. fish*
fruit Obst *n. ohpst*
grapes Weintrauben *pl. vine'-trowb-en*
ham Schinken *m. shink'-en*
ice-cream Eis *n.,* Eiscreme *m. ice, ice'-kraym*
jam Marmelade *f.,* Konfitüre *f.*
    *mahr-me-lahd'-*e, *kon-fee-t*EEr*'-*e
lemon Zitrone *f. tsee-trohn'-*e

E   65

Food and Wine

lobster Hummer *m. hoomm'-er*
marmalade Orangenmarmelade *f.*
           oh-rahn'-she-mahr-me-lahd'-e
melon Melone *f. may-lohn'-e*
mushrooms Pilze *pl. pilts'-e*
mussels Muschel *f. moosh'-el*
mustard Mostrich *m. mohst'-rik*, Senf *m. senf*
oil Öl *n. erl*
onions Zwiebeln *pl. tsveeb'-eln*
orange Apfelsine *f. ahp'-fel-see'-ne*
oysters Austern *pl. owst'-ern*
parsley Petersilie *f. payt-er-zeel'-ye*
peach Pfirsich *f. pfeer'-sik*
pear Birne *f. beern'-e*
peas Erbsen *pl. airp'-sen*
pepper Pfeffer *m. pfeff'-er*
pork Schweinefleisch *n. shvine'-e-fly'sh*
potatoes Kartoffeln *pl. kart-off'-eln*
poultry Geflügel *n. ge-flEEg'-el*
rice Reis *m. rice*
roll Brötchen *n. brert'-ken*
salad Salat *m. sahl-aht'*
salt Salz *n. sahlts*
sauce Sosse *f. soh'-sse*
scampi Skampi *pl. skahm'-pee*
shrimps Krabben *pl. Krahbb'-en*
soup Suppe *f. soopp'-e*
sugar Zucker *m. tsoock'-er*
toast Toast *m. tohst*
tomatoes Tomaten *pl. toh-maht'-en*
vanilla Vanille *f. vahn-eel'-ye*

veal Kalbfleisch *n.* *kahlp'-fly'sh*
vegetables Gemüse *n.* *ge-mEES'-e*
vinegar Essig *m.* *ess'-i*k

DRINKS

aperitif Aperitif *m.* *ah-pair-ee-teef'*
beer Bier *n.* *beer*
brandy Kognak *m.* *kon'-yahk*
chocolate Schokolade *f.* *shoh-koh-lahd'-e*
coffee Kaffee *m.* *kahff'-ay*
gin Gin *m.* *shin*
ice Eis *n.* *ice*
lemonade Limonade *f.* *lee-moh-nahd'-e*
liqueur Likör *m.* *le-ker'*
milk Milch *f.* *milk*
mineral water Mineralwasser *n.* *min'-er-ahl-vahss-er*
orangeade Orangeade *f.* *oh-rahn-shahd'-e*
port Portwein *m.* *port'-vine*
rum Rum *m.* *room*
sherry Sherry *m.* *sherr'-ee*
soda water Sodawasser *n.* *soh'-dah-vahss-er*
tea Tee *m.* *tay*
water Wasser *n.* *vahss'-er*
whisky Whisky *m.* *viss'-kee*
wine Wein *m.* *vine*

USEFUL PHRASES FOR THE RESTAURANT

May I (we) have a table?   Kann ich (Können wir)
                                einen Tisch haben?
*kahn i*k *(kern'-en veer) ine'-en tish hahb'-en*

May I (we) have a snack?	Kann ich (Können wir) einen Imbiss haben?
*kahnn i*k (*kernn'-en veer*) *ine'-en im'-biss hahb'-en*	
I am (We are) in a hurry	Ich bin (Wir sind) in Eile
ik bin (veer sint) in i'-le	
May I (we) have a menu?	Kann ich (Können wir) die Speisekarte haben?
*kahnn i*k (*kernn'-en veer*) *de shpys'-e-kahrt-e hahb'-en*	
Have you any English dishes?	Gibt es irgendwelche englische Gerichte?
gibt ess eerg'-ent-velk-e aing'-lish-e ge-rikt'-e	
I like it well done (medium, underdone)	Ich möchte es gut durch (mittel, roh) haben
ik merkt'-e ess goot doork' (mitt'-el, roh) hahb'-en	
May I (we) have some bread?	Kann ich (Können wir) etwas Brot bekommen?
*kahnn i*k (*kernn'-en veer*) *et'-vahs broht be-kom'-en*	
I (we) will have the set lunch (dinner)	Ich will (Wir wollen) ein festes Menu (eine Mahlzeit) bestellen
ik vill (veer voll'-en) ine fayst'-ess me-nee' (ine'-e mahl'-tsite) be-shtell'-en	
A little more	Ein bisschen mehr
ine bis'-ken mair	
That is enough	Das genügt
duss ge-neegt'	
May I (we) have a (half) bottle of dry (sweet) wine?	Kann ich (Können wir) eine (halbe) Flasche herben (süssen) Wein haben?
*kahnn i*k (*kernn'-en veer*) *ine'-e (hahlb'-e) flahsh'-e hairb'-en (sees'-sen) vine hahb'-en*	

68

May I (we) have some water?	Kann ich (Können wir) etwas Wasser haben?

kahnn ik (kernn'-en veer) et'-vahs vahss'-er hahb'-en

May I (we) have some coffee?	Kann ich (Können wir) etwas Kaffee haben?

kahnn ik (kernn'-en veer) et'-vahs kahff'-ay hahb'-en

May I (we) have a pot of (strong) tea?	Kann ich (Können wir) eine Kanne (starken) Tee haben?

kahnn ik (kernn'-en veer) ine'-e kahn'-ne (shtahr'-ken) tay hahb'-en

I do not like fat	Ich will kein Fett

ik vill kine fet

What do you recommend?	Was würden Sie empfehlen?

vohss veerd'-en see emp-fail'-en

Would you bring the cruet?	Können Sie uns Salz und Pfeffer bringen?

kernn'-en see oonns sahlts oond pfef'-er bring'-en

May I have some butter?	Kann ich etwas Butter haben?

kahnn ik et'-vahss boott'-er hahb'-en

May I have some ice?	Kann ich etwas Eis haben?

kahnn ik et'-vahss ice hahb'-en

Would you bring me an ash-tray?	Würden Sie mir bitte einen Aschenbecher bringen?

veerd'-en see meer bitt'-e ine'-en ahsh'-en-bek-er bring'-en

I will come back	Ich werde wiederkommen

ik vaird'-e veed'-er-kom-en

May I reserve a table for tonight?	Kann ich einen Tisch für heute abend reservieren?

kahnn ik ine'-en tish fEEr hoyt'-e ahb'-ent ray-sair-veer'-en

May I have the bill?	Kann ich die Rechnung haben?
kahnn ik de rek'-noong hahb'-en	
The meal was excellent	Es hat sehr gut geschmeckt
ess hahtt sair goot ge-shmeckt'	

Shopping

English is spoken in most shops in the larger towns and tourist centres. Opening hours are usually from 8 or 8.30 a.m. to 6.30 p.m. Monday to Friday. On the first Saturday each month shops close at 6 p.m.; on other Saturdays at 2 p.m. Hairdressers do not open on Mondays. Local bye-laws may alter these times.

There is, of course, a great variety of goods available; optical equipment is very good value in the higher price range, although most tourists will want humbler souvenirs. Glassware and porcelain make ideal purchases (although the centres of these industries, Bohemia and Dresden, are now in East Germany, the traditions have been carried on in the west). You can buy beautiful wax candles from Nuremburg, and Black Forest cuckoo clocks are obvious souvenirs. Many of the regional food and wine specialities make ideal gifts; marzipan from Lübeck, Nuremberg and Aachen gingerbreads, cherry and raspberry brandies from the Black Forest, and the sweet liqueurs produced in the Bavarian monasteries.

If you are motoring or camping and you feel like a picnic there is a variety of palate-tingling food available, either from the self-service stores to be found in most towns or from the little village shop. A bottle of local wine, minerals, fresh rolls and butter, and an endless choice of cold meats and sausages, delectable cheeses and fruit will enable you to make up a marvellous picnic to be eaten when and whever you feel inclined.

USEFUL WORDS AND PHRASES

(Many foodstuffs will be found listed under the FOOD AND WINE section.)

GENERAL

belt Gürtel *m.* *gEErt'*-el
blouse Bluse *f.* *blooz'*-e
book Buch *n.* *book*
bracelet Armband *n.* *ahrm'*-bahnt
braces Hosenträger *pl.* *hohs'*-en-trayg-er
brassiere Büstenhalter *m.* *bEEst'*-en-hahlt-er
brooch Brosche *f.* *brosh'*-e
buttons Knöpfe *pl.* *knerpf'*-e
cap Kappe *f.* *kahpp'*-e
cigars Zigarren *pl.* *tsee-gahrr'*-en
cigarettes Zigaretten *pl.* *tsee-gah-rett'*-en
coat Mantel *m.* *mahnt'*-el
dictionary Wörterbuch *n.* *vert'*-er-book
doll Puppe *f.* *poop'*-e
dress Kleid *n.* *klit*e
earrings Ohrringe *pl.* *ohr'*-ing-e
elastic Gummi *m.* *goomm'*-ee
envelopes Umschläge *pl.* *oom'*-shlay-ge

gloves Handschuhe *pl. hahnt'-shoo-h*e

gramophone record Grammophonplatte *f.*
                    grahm-moh-fohn'-plahtt-e

guide book Reiseführer *m. ry'-ze-fEER-er*

handbag Handtasche *f. hahnd'-tuhsh-e*

handkerchiefs Taschentücher *pl. tahsh'-en-tEEk-er*

hat Hut *m. hoot*

ink Tinte *f. tin'-te*

jacket Jacke *f. yack'-e*

jumper Jumper *m. shahmp'-er*

lace Spitze *f.,* Borte *f. shpit'-se, bohr'-t*e

lighter Zigarettenanzünder *m.*
                    tsee-gah-rett'-en-ahn-tsEEn-der

lighter flint Feuerstein *m. foy'-er-shtine*

lighter fuel Feuerung (— Benzin)
                foy'-er-oong (bent-seen')

map Landkarte *f. lahnd'-kahr-t*e

matches Streichhölzer *pl. shtry'k'-herlt-ser*

necklace Halskette *f, hahlls'-kett-e*

needle Nadel *f. nahd'-el*

newspaper Zeitung *f. tsite'-oong*

nightdress Nachthemd *n. nahkt'-haymd*

nylons Nylon-Strümpfe *pl. ny'-lon-shtrEEmpf-e*

pants Schlüpfer *pl. shleep'-fair*

pen Federhalter *m. fay'-der-hahllt-er*

pencil Bleistift *m. bly'-shtift*

petticoat Unterrock *m. oont'-er-rock*

pipe Pfeife *f. p'fife'-e*

pin Stecknadel *f. shteck'-nahd-el*

pullover Pullover *m. pooll-oh-ver'*

purse Geldbeutel *m. gelt'-boyt-el*

pyjamas Schlafanzug *m. shlahf'-ahnts-oog*
ring Ring *m. ringk*
sandals Sandalen *pl. sahn-dahl'-en*
scarf Schal *m.* Halstuch *n. shahl, hahls'-took*
scissors Schere *f. shair'-e*
shawl Umhängetuch *n. oom'-heng-e-took*
shirt Hemd *n. hemd*
shoes Schuhe *pl. shoo'-e*
shoe polish Schuhwichse *m. shoo'-vick-se*
shoe laces Schuhbänder *pl. shoo'-bend-er*
silk Seide *f. sy'-de*
skirt Rock *m. rock*
slip (halbes) Unterkleid *n. (hahlb'-es) oont'-er-klite*
slippers Pantoffeln *pl. pahnt-off'-eln*
soap Seife *f. sy'-fe*
socks Socken *pl. sock'-en*
spectacles Brille *f. brill'-e*
stockings Strümpfe *pl. shtrEEmpf'-e*
strap Riemen *m.* Band *n. ree'-men, bahnt*
string Bindfaden *m. bint'-fahd-en*
suit Anzug *m.,* Kostüm *n. ahn'-tsoog, kost-EEm'*
suitcase Koffer *m. koff'-er*
thread Faden *m. fahd'-en*
tie Schlips *m. shlips*
tobacco Tabak *m. tah'-bahk*
tobacco pouch Tabacksbeutel *m. tah'-bahks-boy'-tel*
toy Spielzeug *n. spheel'-tsoyk*
trousers Hosen *pl. hohs'-en*
umbrella (Regen)Schirm *m. (ray'-ghen) sheerm*
undies Unterwäsche *f. oont'-er-vesh-e*
wallet Brieftasche *f. breef'-tahsh-e*

watch Uhr *f. oor*
wool Wolle *f. voll'-e*
writing paper Schreibpapier *n. shripe'-pah-peer*

I want to buy a ...	Ich möchte ein (eine, einen) ... kaufen
ik merkt'-e ine (ine'-e, ine'-en) ... kowf'-en	
How much is this?	Wie teuer ist das?
vee toy'-er ist duss	
Will you show me some ...?	Können Sie mir etwas ... zeigen?
kernn'-en see meer et'-vahs ... tsy'-gen	
Have you anything cheaper (dearer)?	Haben Sie etwas billigeres (teueres)?
hahb'-en see et'-vahs bill'-eeg-er-ess (toy'-er-ess)	
Have you anything bigger (smaller)?	Haben Sie etwas grösseres (kleineres)?
hahb'-en see et'-vahs grer'-ser-es (kly'-ner-es)	
Do you have it in other colours?	Haben Sie es in anderen Farben?
hahb'-en see ess in ahn'-der-en fahr'-ben	
Will you deliver it?	Können Sie es mir schicken?
kernn'-en see ess meer shick'-en	
I will collect it later	Ich werde es später abholen
ik vaird'-e ess shpay'-ter ahp'-hohl-en	
That's what I want	Das ist genau, was ich will
duss ist ge-now', vahs ik vill	
It is not suitable	Das ist nicht das richtige
duss ist nikt duss rik'-teeg-e	

Could you put it in a box for me?	Könnten Sie mir das in einen Kasten einpacken?

kernnt'-en see meer duss in ine'-en kahst'-en ine'-pahk-en

May I have a receipt?	Könnte ich eine Bescheinigung haben?

kernn'-te ik ine'-e be-shine'-eeg-oong hahb'-en

Can you let me have it by . . . ?	Könnten Sie mir das bis zum . . . verschaffen?

kernnt'-en see meer duss bis tsoom . . . fair-shahff'-en

May I try it (them)?	Kann ich das (diese) anprobieren?

kahnn ik duss (dee'-ze) ahn'-proh-beer-en

Can you repair this?	Können Sie mir das reparieren?

kernn'-en see meer duss ray-pah-reer'-en

Can you have this invisibly mended?	Können Sie mir das kunst-stopfen?

kernn'-en see meer duss koonst'-stopf-en

How long will it take?	Wie lange würde es dauern?

vee lahng'-e veerd'-e duss dow'-ern

THE CHEMIST   **Apotheker** (*ah-poh-tay'-ker*)

aspirin Aspirin *n. ahs-pir-een'*
bandage Verband *m. fair-bahnd'*
bath salts Badesalze *pl. bah'-de-salts-e*
cotton wool Watte *f. vahtt'-e*
face powder Gesichtspuder *ge-sikts'-poo-der*
gargle Gurgelwasser *n. goor-'gel-vahss-er*

laxative Abführmittel *n.* *ahp'-fEER-mitt-el*
lint Lein *m.*, Mull *m.* *line, mooll*
lipstick Lippenstift *m.* *lip'-pen-shtift*
medicine Medizin *f.* *may-de-tseen'*
ointment Salbe *f.* *sahl'-be*
plaster Pflaster *n.* *pflahst'-er*
razor blades Rasierklingen *pl.* *rah-zeer'-kling-en*
sanitary towels Binden *pl.* *bin'-Den*
scissors Schere *f.* *shay'-re*
soap Seife *f.* *sy'-fe*
sunglasses Sonnenbrille *f.* *son'-nen-brill-e*
sun-tan lotion Sonnenöl *n.* *son'-nen-erl*
talcum powder Talkumpuder *m.* *tahl'-koom-poo-der*
throat pastilles Halstabletten *pl.* *hahls'-tahb-lett-en*
toilet paper Toilettenpapier *n.* *toy-lett'-en-pah-peer*

Can you make up this   Können Sie mir dieses
prescription?   Rezept bereiten?
    kern'-en see meer deez'-es re-tsept' be-ry'-ten
My stomach is upset   Ich habe einen verdorbenen
                         Magen
    ik hahb'-e ine'-en fair-dohr'-ben-en mah'gen
I have a ...   Ich habe ...
    ik hahb'-e
Headache. Toothache   Kopfschmerzen.
                         Zahnschmerzen
    kopf'-schmairts-en. tsahn'-schmairts-en
Indigestion. Diarrhoea   Verdauungsmangel.
                         Durchfall
    fair-dow'-oonngs-mahng-el. doork'-fahll

I have been sunburnt Ich hab einen Sonnenbrand
ik hahb'-e ine'-en son'-nen-brahnnt

My feet are blistered Meine Füsse sind voller
Blasen
mine'-e fEESS'-e sint vohll'-er blahs'-en

I want something for insect bites Ich möchte etwas gegen
Insektenbisse
ik merkt'-e et'-vahs gayg'-en in-zekt'-en-bis-e

I think it is poisoned Ich glaube es ist vergifted
ik glow'-be, ess ist fair-gift'-et

I have a head cold Ich bin erkältet
ik bin air-kelt'-et

My throat is very sore Ich habe grosse
Halsschmerzen
ik hahb'-e grohss'-e hahls'-shmairts-en

HAIRDRESSERS **Frisör** *(free-zer')*

appointment Verabredung *f. fair-ahp'-raid-oong*
bleach Bleiche *f. bly'-ke*
brush Bürste *f. bEErs'-te*
colour rinse Farbmittel *n. fahrb'-mitt-el*
comb Kamm *m. kahm*
cut Schnitt *m. shnitt*
manicure Maniküre *f. mah-nee-kEEr'-e*
perm Dauerwelle *f. dow'-er-vell-e*
set Frisur *f. free-zoor'*
shampoo Haarwaschmittel *n. hahr'-vahsh-mitt-e*
tint Farbe *f. fahr'-be*
wave Welle *f. vell'-e*

77

May I make an appointment?	Kann ich eine Verabredung machen?

kah ik ine'-e fair-ahp'-raid-oong mahk-'en

I want a shave	Ich muss mich rasieren lassen

ik mooss mik rah-zeer'-en lahss'-en

I want a haircut	Ich muss mir die Haare schneiden lassen

ik mooss meer de hahr'-e shnide'-en lahss'-en

Not too short	Nicht zu kurz

nikt tsoo koorts

I would like it short	Ich möchte es kurz

ik merk'-te ess koorts

I want a shampoo and set	Ich möchte meine Haare gewaschen und frisiert haben

ik merk'-te mine'-e hahr'-e ge-vahsh'-en oond free-zeert' hahb'-en

It is too hot (cold)	Es ist zu heiss (kalt)

ess ist tsoo hice (kahlt)

It is not dry	Es ist nicht trocken

ess ist nikt trock'-en

That is excellent	Das ist sehr schön so

duss ist sair shern soh

THE PHOTOGRAPHIC SHOP   **Das Photogeschäft**
                              (*duss foh'-toh-ge-shayft*)

black and white film schwarz-weisser Film *m.*
                              shvahrts-vice'-er film
camera Kamera *f. kahm'-er-ah*
colour film Farbfilm *m. fahrb'-film*
develop entwickeln *ent-vick'-eln*
enlarge vergrössern *fair-grers'-ern*
enlargement Vergrösserung *f. fair-grers'-er-oong*
exposure meter Belichtungsmesser *f.*
                              bel-ikt'-oongs-mess-er
filter Filter *m. filt'-er*
glossy glänzend *glent'-send*
lens Linse *f. lin'-ze*
lens hood Linsen-Haube *f. lin'-zen how'-be*
matt matt *mahtt*
negative Negatif *n. nay'-gaht-eef*
print kopieren *koh-peer'-en*
range-finder Entfernungsmesser *m.*
                  ent-fair'-noongs-mess-er
shutter Verschluss *m. fair-shlooss'*
viewfinder Sucher *m. sook'-er*
tripod Stativ *m. shtah-teef'*

Will you develop (and   Bitte entwickeln (und
print) this film?   kopieren) Sie diesen Film
  bitt'-e ent-vick'-eln (oond kohp-eer'-en) see deez'-en film'

I would like some prints (enlargements)   Ich möchte gern einige Drucke (Vergrösserungen)
> *ik merkt'-e gairn ine'-eeg-e droock'-e*
> *(fair-grers'-er-oong-en)*

When will they be ready?   Wann werden sie fertig sein?
> *vahnn vaird'-en see fairt'-ig sine*

The film won't turn   Der Film dreht sich nicht
> *dair film drayt sik nikt*

Do you repair cameras?   Reparieren Sie Kameras?
> *ray-pah-reer'-en see kahm'-er-ahs*

There is something wrong with my camera   Meine Kamera ist kaputt
> *mine'-e kahm'-er-ah isst kahpp-oott'*

OTHER SHOPS

baker Bäckerei *f. beck-e-ry'*
butcher Fleischerei *f.*, Schlächterei *f.*
> *fly-she-ry', shlekt-e-ry'*

cake shop Konditorei *f. kon-dee-toh-ry'*
cleaner Reinigung *f. ry'-ne-goong*
dairy Milchgeschäft *n. milk'-ge-sheft*
delicatessen Delikatessenhandlung *f.*
> *day-le-kaht-ess'-en-hahnd-loong*

draper Tuchhandlung *f. took'-hahnd-loong*
fishmonger Fischgeschäft *n. fish'-ge-sheft*
fruiterer Obsthandlung *f. ohpst'-hahnd-loong*
grocer Kolonialwarenhandlung *f.*
> *kol-on-e-ahl'-vahr-en-hahnd-loong*

ironmonger Eisenhandlung *f. ize'-en-hahnd-loong*
newsagent Zeitungsgeschäft *n. tsite'-oongs-ge-sheft*

perfumery Parfümerie *f. pahr-f*EE*-mer-ee'*
shoe repairer Schuster *m. shoost'-er*
shoe shop Schuhgeschäft *n. shoo'-ge-sheft*
stationer Papierhandlung *f. pah-peer'-hahnd-loong*

Sport, The Beach

Whatever your sport and wherever you may be in Germany you will find no lack of facilities. On the lakes of Hanover, Hesse and Bavaria you can indulge in every aquatic sport, while in the surrounding forests you can hunt chamois and wild boar. Hillside trails along the banks of the Rhine and well-marked paths across the countryside offer excellent possibilities for walkers to fully enjoy the scenic beauty of the regions.

Most holiday resorts have public tennis courts and swimming pools, and there are about 60 golf courses – a quarter of these have 18 holes. There are over 300 winter resorts where you can ski, skate, sleigh-ride or watch ice-hockey and other snow sports.

Canoeing is very popular; the rivers Weser, Main, Neckar and Moselle run through beautiful scenery, while the Bavarian rivers are for experienced canoeists only.

On the North Sea and Baltic coasts there are numerous seaside resorts, some fashionable, some more rustic in character. The climate is relatively mild and balanced and here amid the glorious sands and white dunes one can enjoy all the pleasures of the beach and benefit from the bracing sea air.

USEFUL WORDS AND PHRASES

bathe baden *bahd'-en*
bathing cap Bademütze *f. bahd'-e-mEEts-e*
bathing costume Badeanzug *m. bahd'-e-ahnts-oog*
bathing cabin Badekabine *f. bahd'-e-kah-been'-e*
bay Bucht *f. bookt*
beach Strand *m. shtrahnt*
boat Boot *n. boht*
buoy Boje *f. boh'-ye*
canoe Kanu *n. kah-noo'*
cliff Klippe *f. klipp'-e*
coast Küste *f. kEEst'-e*
current Strömung *f. shtrer'-moong*
deckchair Liegestuhl *m. leeg'-e-shtool*
diving board Sprungbrett *n. shproong'-brett*
fish Fisch *m. fish*
flippers Ruderschwänze *pl.,* Flossen *pl.*
    rood'-er-shvents-e, flohss'-en
jelly-fish Seenesse *f. say'-ness-e*
motorboat Motorboot *n. moh'-tohr-boht*
pebbles Kieselsteine *pl. kee'-zel-shtine-e*
raft Floss *m. flohss*
rocks Felsen *m. fel'-zen*
rowing boat Ruderboot *n. rood'-er-boht*
sailing boat Segelboot *n. say'-gel-boht*

sand Sand *m.* *sahnnt*

sandhills Sandhügel *pl.* *sahnnt'-hEEg-el*

shell Muschel *f.* *moosh'-el*

snorkel Snorkel *m.* *snohr'-kel*

sunshade Sonnenschirm *m.* *sohn'-nen-sheerm*

tide Ebbe und Flut *f.*, Flut *f.* *eb'-e oond floot, floot*

water skis Wasserskis *pl.* *vahss'-er-skees*

wave Welle *f.* *vell'-e*

Bathing prohibited   Baden verboten
         bahd'-en fair-boht'-en

Can I hire a . . . ?   Kann ich ein (eine,
                    einen) . . . mieten?
     kann ik ine (ine'-e, ine'-en) . . . meet'-en

Where is it safe to bathe?   Wo kann man mit
                    Sicherheit baden?
     voh kahnn mahn mit sik'-er-hite bahd'-en

Can I go fishing?   Kann ich angeln gehen?
     kahnn ik ahn'-geln gay'-en

I am not a good swimmer   Ich bin kein guter
                    Schwimmer
     ik bin kine goot'-er shvim'-er

Where can I go   Wo kann ich wasserski-
water-skiing?   laufen
     voh kahnn ik vahss'-er-skee-lowf-en

Is it deep there?   Ist es tief hier?
     ist ess teef heer

Is it safe?	Ist es ungefährlich?
	ist ess oon'-ge-fair-lik
Is it dangerous?	Ist es gefährlich?
	ist ess ge-fair-'lik
I only want to sunbathe	Ich möchte nur sonnenbaden
	ik merkt'-e noor sohn'-nen-bahd-en
Are there any rocks there?	Sind hier irgendwelche Felsen?
	sint heer eer'-gent-velk-e fel'-zen
Does it shelve quickly?	Wird es hier schnell abschüssig?
	veerd ess heer shnell ahp'-shEES-ig
Is there a shower?	Gibt es hier eine Dusche?
	ghibt ess heer ine'-e doosh'-e

Post Office, Telephones

In the main post offices there is usually a clerk with a knowledge of English and the visitor should encounter few difficulties with his transactions, for some of which he may have to produce his passport. Letter boxes are painted yellow and are frequently built into the wall. When using a non-automatic telephone box, dictate the number you require in pairs of numbers; 30 21 06 is thus said "dreissig, einundzwanzig, null sechs" (thirty, twenty-one, nil six, not three oh two one oh six).

In emergencies, dial 110 for traffic accidents and 112 for first aid, ambulance or fire alarm. In smaller places these numbers may be different; they will be found listed on the cover of the telephone directory, under "Notrufe" (emergencies) or "Wichtige Telefon-Nummern" (important telephone numbers). You cannot obtain these emergency services from public call boxes without inserting coins. Keep a small supply of 10 Pfennig coins handy; these will be useful for local calls (20 Pfg from call boxes) and parking meters.

USEFUL WORDS AND PHRASES

cablegram Kabeltelegramm *n. kahb'-el-tay-le-grahm*

call Telefonanruf *m. tay-le-fohn'-ahn-roof*

call box Telefonkiosk *m. tay-le-fohn'-ke-osk*

collection (Brief) Leerung *f. (breef) lay'-roong*

directory Telefonbuch *n. tay-le-fohn'-book*

international money order Auslandspostanweisung *m.*
                     owss'-lahnts-posst'-ahn-vy-zoong

letter Brief *m. breef*

letter-box Briefkasten *m. breef'-kahsst-en*

number Nummer *f. noom'-er*

parcel Paket *n. pah-kait'*

post card Postkarte *f. posst'-kahrt-e*

post office Postamt *n. posst'-ahmt*

postal order Postanweisung *m. posst'-ahn-vy-zoong*

stamp Briefmarke *f.* *breef'-marke-e*

telegram Telegramm *n.* *tay'-le-grahm*

telephone Telefon *n.* *tay'-le-fohn,*
Fernsprecher *m.* *fairn'-sphrek-er*

to telephone telefonieren *tay-le-fohn-eer'-en*
anrufen *ahn'-roof-en*

Where is the nearest post   Wo ist das nächste Postamt
office (telephone)?   (Telefon)?
    voh ist duss naykst'-e pohst'-ahmt (tay'-le-fohn)

Where is the nearest   Wo ist der nächste
letter-box?   Briefkasten?
    voh ist der naykst'-e breef'-kahsst-en

I want to send this   Ich will diese Postkarte
post-card (letter, parcel)   (diesen Brief, dieses Paket)
    abschicken
    ik vill dee'-ze pohst'-kahrt-e (dee'-zen breef,
    dee'-zes pah-kait') ahp'-shik-en

I want to register this letter   Ich will diesen Brief
    registrieren
    ik vill dee'-zen breef ray-gist-treer'-en

Are there any letters for me?   Ist Post für mich da?
    ist pohst fEER mik dah

Is there a parcel for me?   Ist ein Paket für mich
    gekommen?
    ist ine pah-kait' fEER mik ge-komm'-en

Here is my passport   Hier ist mein Pass
    heer ist mine pahss

Medical Services

Under the EEC Social Security regulations visitors from the UK qualify for treatment on the same basis as West Germans themselves. But you must remember to complete the form CM1 (obtainable from your own Social Security office or employment exchange) at least six months before travelling. This will enable you to be issued with the necessary certificate (E111), and you will also get an explanatory leaflet concerning free or cheap treatment within the Common Market countries.

USEFUL WORDS AND PHRASES

accident Unfall *m. oon'-fahl*
ambulance Krankenwagen *m. krahnk'-en-vahg-en*
appendicitis Blinddarmentzündung *f.*
        *blinnt'-darm-ent-ts*EEN*d-oong*
bandage Verband *m. fair-bahnd'*
bite Biss *m. bis*
blister Blase *f. blahs'-*e
burn Verbrennung *f. fair-bren-'oong*
chill Verkühlung *f. fair-k*EEL*'-oong*
constipation Verstopfung *f. fair-shtohpf'-oong*
cough Husten *m. hoost'-*en
cramp Krampf *m. krahmpf*
cut Schnitt *m. shnit*
dentist Zahnarzt *m. tsahn'-ahrtst*
diarrhoea Durchfall *m. doork'-fahl*
doctor Arzt *m. ahrtst*
faint Ohnmacht *f. ohn'-mahkt*
fever Fieber *n. feeb'-*er

filling (Zahn) füllung *f.* (*tsahn*) *f*EE*ll'-oong*

fracture Bruch *m. brook*

hospital Krankenhaus *n. krahnk'-en-hows*

indigestion Verdauungsmangel *n.*
              fair-dow'-oongs-mahng-el

influenza Influenza *f. in-floo-ents'-ah*

insomnia Schlaflosigkeit *f. shlahf'-loh-sig-kite*

injection Spritze *f. shprits'-e*

nurse Schwester *f.*, Krankenschwester *f.*
        shvest'-er, krahnk'-en-shvest-er

pain Schmerz *m. shmairts*

poison Vergiftung *f. fair-gif'-toong*

policeman Polizist *m: poh-le-tsist'*

sick krank *krahnk*

sling Schlinge *f. shling'-e*

splint Schiene *f. sheen'-e*

sprain Verrenkung *f. fair-renk'-oong*

sting Stich *m. shtik*

stomach-ache Magenschmerz *m. mahg'-en-shmairts*
               Bauchschmerz *m, bowk'-shmairts*

sunstroke Sonnenstich *m. sohn'-nen-shtik*

surgery Sprechstunde *f. shprek'-shtoond-e*

temperature Temperatur *f. temp-e-rah-toor'*

throat Hals *m. hahls*

toothache Zahnschmerz *m. tsann'-shmairts*

to vomit (sich) übergeben (*sik*) EE-*ber-gayb'-en*

Call an ambulance (policeman) quickly Rufen Sie sofort einen Kranken-wagen (einen Polizisten)

roof'-en see soh-fohrt' ine'-en krahnk'-en-vahg-en (ine'-en pohl-e-tsist'-en)

Stand back Machen Sie Platz!

mak'-en see plahts

Give him (her) air Geben Sie ihm (ihr) Luft!

gay'-ben see eem (eer) looft

Is there a doctor near here? Ist ein Doktor in der Nähe?

ist ine dok'-tohr in dair nay'-e

Have you a bandage? Haben Sie einen Verband?

habv'-en see ine'-en fair-bahnd'

Bring some hot (cold) water Bringen Sie heisses (kaltes) Wasser

brin'-gen see hice'-ess (kahlt'-es) vahss'-er

Bring me a blanket Geben Sie mir eine Decke

gay'-ben see meer ine'-e deck'-e

Do not move him (her) Bewegen Sie ihn (sie) nicht

be-vayg'-en see een (see) nikt

Do you have any pain here? Haben Sie irgendwelche Schmerzen hier?

hahb'-en see ir'-gent-velk-e shmairts'-en heer

I have a pain here Ich habe hier Schmerzen

ik hahb'-e heer shmairts'-en

Where is the nearest dentist? Wo wohnt der nächste Zahnarzt?

voh vohnt dair nai̇kst'-e tsahn'-ahrst

Will you give me an injection? Können Sie mir eine Spritze geben?

kernn'-en see meer ine'-e shprits'-e gay-ben

Useful Information

Currency, Banks

There is no limit to the amount of foreign currency that a visitor may bring into or take out of the Federal Republic. Many German shops and hotels will accept payment in foreign currency notes. Exchange facilities are to be found at banks, frontier posts, railway stations, travel bureaux and hotels. Banks generally open from 8.30 a.m. until 1 p.m. and from 2.30 until 4 p.m. They are closed on Saturdays. When cashing travellers' cheques you must produce your passport.

The unit of German money is the Deutsche Mark (or D Mark, pronounced *day-mark*). 1 DM = 100 Pfennigs. You are asked to insert below the prevailing rate of exchange, as this is subject to some fluctuation.

10 Pfennigs =	20 D Marks =
50 Pfennigs =	50 D Marks =
1 D Mark =	100 D Marks =
5 D Marks=	500 D Marks =

Tipping

Although a service charge is included in all bills in hotels and restaurants it is usual to add to this any small change. Tip taxi-drivers and porters as in Britain.

Interpreters and Guides

Local tourist offices and travel agencies in all principal centres can supply reliable guides and interpreters at a reasonable fee, who will show visitors around and explain to them all the interesting things they see. At hotels, important museums and other places of interest there are usually members of the staff who speak foreign languages and are therefore able to help you in every way.

Tourist Offices

Detailed information is available, while you are travelling in Germany, from all local tourist agencies as well as the following regional tourist associations (the abbreviations LVV and FVV stand for Lands- or Fremden-Verkehrsband). Note the use of German spelling for towns and regions—München = Munich, etc.:

FVV Schleswig-Holstein, Adelheidstr. 10, 23 Kiel.

FVV Nordsee-Niedersachsen-Bremen Gottorpstr. 18, 29 Oldenburg.

FVV Lüneburger Heide, Rathaus, 314 Lüneburg.

LVV Westfalen, Balkenstr. 4, 46 Dortmund.

LVV Weserbergland-Mittelweser, Falkenstr. 2, 325 Hameln.

Harzer Verkehrsverband, Marktstr. 45, 338 Goslar.

Fremdenverkehrszentrale Hamburg, Bieberhaus am Hauptbahnhof, 2 Hamburg 1.

LVV Hessen, Bismarckring 23, 62 Wiesbaden.

Verkehrsamt Berlin, Fasanenstr. 7-8, 1 Berlin 12.

FVV Rheinland, Rheinallee 69, 533 Bonn-Bad Godesberg.

FVV Rheinland-Pfalz, Hochhaus, 54 Koblenz.

FVV Saarland, Haus Berlin, 66 Saarbrücken.

FVV Nordbaden, Rathaus, 69 Heidelberg.

FVV Württemberg, Charlottenplatz 17, 7 Stuttgart.

FVV Schwarzwald-Bodensee, Bismarckallee 6, 78 Freiburg.

FVV Nordbayern, Am Plärrer 14, 85 Nürnberg.

FVV Ostbayern, Richard Wagner Str. 10, 84 Regensburg.

FVV München-Oberbayern, Sonnenstr. 10, 8 München.

FVV Schwaben-Allgäu, Halderstr. 12, 89 Augsburg.

Public Conveniences

These are few and far between outside the larger cities, though one can use the facilities of a local restaurant or bar without necessarily buying anything.

May I use your lavatory, please?	Kann ich Ihre Toilette benutzen?

kahnn ik *ee'-re twah-lett'-e be-noot'-sen*

British and Continental Clothing

Dresses and suits (Women)   *Junior Miss*

British	34	36	38	40	42	44		32	33	35	36	38	39
Continental	40	42	44	46	48	50		38	40	42	44	46	48

Men's suits

British	36	38	40	42	44	46
Continental	46	48	50	52	54	56

Shirts and Collars

British	14	$14\frac{1}{2}$	15	$15\frac{1}{2}$	16	$16\frac{1}{2}$	17
Continental	36	37	38	39	41	42	43

Shoes

British	3	4	5	6	7	8	9	10	11	12
Continental	36	37	38	39	41	42	43	44	46	47

Hats

British	$6\frac{1}{2}$	$6\frac{5}{8}$	$6\frac{3}{4}$	$6\frac{7}{8}$	7	$7\frac{1}{8}$	$7\frac{1}{4}$	$7\frac{3}{8}$	$7\frac{1}{2}$
Continental	53	54	55	56	57	58	59	60	61

Stockings

British	8	$8\frac{1}{2}$	9	$9\frac{1}{2}$	10	$10\frac{1}{2}$
Continental	0	1	2	3	4	5

Socks

British	$9\frac{1}{2}$	10	$10\frac{1}{2}$	11	$11\frac{1}{2}$
Continental	38-39	39-40	40-41	41-42	42-43

Gloves are the same size as in Britain.

Electric Current

This is usually 220 volts A.C. but in some places it is 110 volts D.C. so your shaver (and other appliances) will need an adaptor.

Conversion Tables

DISTANCES

Distances are marked in kilometres. To convert kilometres to miles, divide the km. by 8 and multiply by 5. Convert miles to km. by dividing the miles by 5 and multiplying by 8. A mile is 1 km. 610 m.

km.	miles *or km.*	miles	km.	miles *or km.*	miles
1·6	1	0·6	16·1	10	6·2
3·2	2	1·2	32·2	20	12·4
4·8	3	1·9	48·3	30	18·6
6·4	4	2·5	64·4	40	24·9
8·1	5	3·1	80·5	50	31·1
9·7	6	3·7	160·9	100	62·1
11·3	7	4·4	321·9	200	124·2
12·9	8	5·0	804·7	500	310·7
14·5	9	5·6	1609·4	1000	621·4

Other units of length:

1 centimetre = 0·39 in.	1 inch = 25·4 millimetres
1 metre = 39·37 in.	1 foot = 0·30 metre (30 cm.)
10 metres = 32·81 ft.	1 yard = 0·91 metre

WEIGHTS

The unit you will come into most contact with is the kilogram or kilo. To convert kg. to lbs., multiply by 2 and add 1/10 of the result. One kilo (1000 gr.) is 2 lb. 3 oz.; one stone is 6·35 kg; one cwt. is 51 kg.

grams	ounces		ounces	grams
50	1·75		1	28·0
100	3·50		2	57·1
250	8·80		4	114·3
500	17·6		8	228·6

kg.	lbs. or kg.	lbs.	kg.	lbs. or kg.	lbs.
0·5	1	2·2	3·6	8	17·6
0·9	2	4·4	4·1	9	19·8
1·4	3	6·6	4·5	10	22·1
1·8	4	8·8	9·1	20	44·1
2·3	5	11·0	11·3	25	55·1
2·7	6	13·2	22·7	50	110·2
3·2	7	15·4	45·4	100	220·5

LIQUIDS

Petrol being sold in litres, the following table (in Imperial gallons) will aid your calculations—remember that while an Imperial gallon is roughly 4½ litres an American gallon is only 3·8 litres. One litre is about 1¾ pints a pint is 0·57 litre.

litres	gals. or l.	gals.	litres	gals. or l.	gals.
4·6	1	0·2	36·4	8	1·8
9·1	2	0·4	40·9	9	2·0
13·6	3	0·7	45·5	10	2·2
18·2	4	0·9	90·9	20	4·4
22·7	5	1·1	136·4	30	6·6
27·3	6	1·3	181·8	40	8·8
31·8	7	1·5	227·3	50	11·0

TYRE PRESSURES

lbs. per sq. inch	17	18	19	20
kg. per sq. cm.	1k 200	1k 250	1k 350	1k 400

lbs. per sq. inch	21	22	23	24
kg. per sq. cm.	1k 475	1k 500	1k 600	1k 700

lbs. per sq. inch	25	26	27	28
kg. per sq. cm.	1k 750	1k 850	1k 900	1k 950